Praise for *Blackthorn's Botanical Brews*

"An absolutely exceptional magical resource that you'll enjoy reading cover to cover! From teas and kombucha, to liquors and liqueurs, and even a few delectable bites, author Amy Blackthorn's zesty, exciting writing and impressive knowledge will inspire your kitchen witchery. For everyone from beginner to advanced practitioner, *Blackthorn's Botanical Brews* will guide you on how to embrace the innate magical potential of everyday libations and inspire you to express and imbibe your own unique approach to magic."

—Julia Halina Hadas, author of *WitchCraft Cocktails:*
70 Seasonal Drinks Infused with Magic and Ritual

"A lighthearted but practical approach to spells, sips, and sensational libations. Amy Blackthorn combines magical working with simple ideas and recipes for potions, herbal teas, and cocktails that hold enough power for your next ritual celebration but are delicious enough to share with friends and family. Amy's knowledge of herbalism and lore gives the practitioner an in-depth understanding of potion-making."

—Dawn Aurora Hunt, owner of Cucina Aurora Kitchen Witchery,
and author of *A Kitchen Witch's Guide to Recipes for Love & Romance*

"Amy Blackthorn has written a book combining the science and magic of mixology. Her recipes for magical intent are a must read for anyone looking to expand their potion and libation abilities."

—Jon Talkington, owner and meadmaker of
The Brimming Horn Meadery

"Filled with helpful potion and spell-building information, *Blackthorn's Botanical Brews* features recipes for delicious infusions and syrups with which to make magical beverages with sober versions thoughtfully included. A fun magical twist to cocktail hour and, of course, for ritual gatherings."

—Kathleen Cowley, magical chocolatière and owner of
Enchanted Chocolates of Martha's Vineyard

"Amy Blackthorn has done it again and done it with luscious writing and a lip-smacking presentation of brews and potions. She takes us through the basics of magic and teases the reader with the tools of this particular craft. *Blackthorn's Botanical Brews* is clever, clear, and—dare I say?—delicious."

—H. Byron Ballard, homebrewer, and author of *Embracing
Willendorf: A Witch's Way of Loving Your Body to Health and Fitness*

"Tea, tonics, cocktails and potions! Have you ever enjoyed an afternoon into its evening, sitting at an old, polished bar, while a careful blender performed their art for you? If you enjoy a good drink—an *accomplished* drink—you will discover many within *Blackthorn's Botanical Brews*. This is a master Book of Shadows for a damn good drink with purpose, penned with knowledge and skillful wort cunning. All the historical bells and mixers are available in this book. What better timing than now for imbibing with witchcraft? "

—Gwendolyn H. Barry, blender and owner of
Daughters of Isis, Inc.

"While revealing the magick in everyday activities such as preparing a cup of tea or mixing a cocktail, Blackthorn expertly anticipates readers' questions and answers them with a grounded understanding of the magickal principles that govern spells and libations. Filled with

clever cocktail recipes, as well as sober solutions, Blackthorn incorporates magickal correspondences for her ingredients that lend power and lore to her lovingly crafted libations. You may never look at a martini glass in quite the same way after taking in Blackthorn's magickal insight on potions. With an elixir for every occasion, expect to be delighted and charmed by this refreshing and original practical guide."
—Judy Ann Nock, author of *The Modern Witchcraft Guide to Magickal Herbs* and other books

"*Blackthorn's Botanical Brews* is an exceptionally good read. I can imagine regularly grabbing this fun, witty, information-rich gem from my cookery and magic bookshelf to make magical cocktails, tisanes, and libations for parties, spells, and magical gatherings of all sorts. Interwoven with the magical mixology runs a thread of well-founded solid magical praxis designed to elucidate, educate, and entertain. For anyone who works their magic with food and drink and herbs, this book is a must have. I give it five out of five cocktail shakers!"
—Gwion Raven, author of *The Magick of Food: Rituals, Offerings & Why We Eat Together*

"Amy Blackthorn makes magic accessible with easy-to-follow recipes, using easily procured ingredients for relatable scenarios. Even the most seasoned of mixologists will be inspired by this delightful collection of cocktails, mocktails, and more."
—Camille Kea, certified hypnotherapist and past-life regressionist, tarotista, and former Oakland Nightlife Examiner at *Examiner.com*

"Amy Blackthorn has concocted an ingenious book. More than just a simple recipe book, *Blackthorn's Botanical Brews* contains the deep understanding, research, and creative cleverness expected from a well-seasoned witch like Blackthorn. Drawing upon the art of witchery's traditional concepts, theories, and tools, Amy applies them to the art of crafting drinks in an imaginative and fun way, transforming ordinary teas, cocktails, and mocktails into powerful potions with formulas that are just as delicious as her insights."

—Mat Auryn, author of *Psychic Witch: A Metaphysical Guide to Meditation, Magick, and Manifestation*

BLACKTHORN'S
BOTANICAL
BREWS

HERBAL POTIONS, MAGICAL TEAS, AND SPIRITED LIBATIONS

AMY BLACKTHORN

WEISER BOOKS

This edition first published in 2020 by Weiser Books, an imprint of
Red Wheel/Weiser, LLC
With offices at:
65 Parker Street, Suite 7
Newburyport, MA 01950
www.redwheelweiser.com

ISBN: 978-1-57863-715-7
Library of Congress Cataloging-in-Publication Data available upon request.

Cover and text design by Kathryn Sky-Peck
Typeset in Minion Pro

Printed in the United States of America
LB
10 9 8 7 6 5

To the Priestesses and Priests of the Bar:
Laura, Peep, Bill, Jon, and John.

Liquors are horticulture, distilled down to its finest form.

Contents

Acknowledgments

To Laura, who never did make fun of the face I made the first time I tried kombucha. To John, king of the room party bartenders and alchemical mixologist. To Jon T., who showed us his art form was blending flavors. Hail, The Brimming Horn Meadery. To Byron, who is always ready to listen, encourage, support, or kick butt, I love you. To Krissy who regaled me with stories of her family's Bloody Mary recipe. To the friends I can share a glass of mead with, tell stories over a horn with, and share our triumphs with, hail Whitemarsh Theod. To my dear friend and editor, Judika Illes, your support and guidance have changed my life into something of my dreams, thank you. To the entire staff of Weiser Books for their unwavering support of my dreams and goals. To Kane and Josh, who always listen, even if they don't always understand what the heck I'm talking about. To my family for their love and support. To Michael K. and Melissa D., two of the best cheerleaders a woman could ask for. For you, the reader. And lastly, to the first priestess and priest of the bar, Peep and Willy—gone but never forgotten.

Introduction

People have been fascinated with the idea of bubbling cauldrons full of magic brews since that old time immemorial. When someone says, "witch," we conjure up images of women—crone, mother, and maiden—standing over bubbling vats of mysterious liquids said to contain the power of the elements, and life itself. However, most books won't touch the subject of potions, for fear of allergies, lawsuits, and unintentional poisonings. This book was written to address this subject head-on, by teaching you, dear reader, not only what potions are, but what purposes they serve, and how to create these brews.

What is a potion? Simply, a drink—a drink reputed to have magical powers and that may be medicinal or sometimes poisonous. After all, what is the difference between medicine and poison? Dosage.

What are some culturally acceptable toxins? Beer, wine, and other alcoholic beverages. Cigars and cigarettes. One drink has a euphoric effect, more drinks induce a depressive state. Too many drinks and we risk alcohol poisoning.

Then there is the magical effect. Each beverage is designed to encourage a different state. Love potions could contain aphrodisiac herbs, while healing tonics contain soothing plants. The magic comes not only from knowing how to prepare each item, but also through imbuing it with our own love and energy to make it magical.

Mom's chicken noodle soup just isn't the same when we make it. We like to think the thing that's missing is the loving feelings Mom would put into it. To take a drink, and make it a potion, we need the extra step.

Are you for real?

I know that the idea of magic can feel odd if you haven't worked with it yet. It sounds like something from a sci-fi/fantasy novel. (Fun fact: Lots of writers of witchcraft nonfiction also write sci-fi/fantasy novels.) It is a common belief that since energy can be neither created nor destroyed, spells are merely changing the form of the energy. For instance, if I need money, I might burn a green candle. The energy I raise (we'll discuss this in a moment) along with the flame of the candle provides fuel to create a change of circumstances. We are changing the energy of the candle into the power of prosperity. Do you need a candle? No. It is pretty helpful, though, especially when you're first starting. It gives you something to focus on, a mental touchstone to remind yourself that you are working on something.

So, you do spells? What kind of things can spells do?

It's common to hear a magical practitioner liken spells to enacted prayers, but that is misleading. Prayers reach out to the divine, and magic can be used with or without a connection to any deity. Magic is directing energy; if you decide to ask for a creator to help lead it, that's up to you. It isn't necessary. What's needed is your belief. That's 90+ percent of the fuel it needs to be successful. The number one killer of all magic is doubt. If you doubt your spells, intentions, or work, that's when the magic starts to fail.

What about God?

What about Him/Her/It/Them? Do witches worship God? Some do. If you can name a mythology or a pantheon, there are likely people alive today worshipping Them. The "old gods" are still just as much a part of the lives of witches as they always were. Hecate, Brighid, Diana, Kali, Innana, they are still alive and well and being worshipped in homes all over the world. There are Christian witches; there are also witches who follow one god, or entire pantheons. There are even atheistic and non-theistic practitioners. The long and short of it is, if you love a witch, ask *them* what they believe. Asking their spouse, mom, brother, or cousin isn't going to give you their whole picture. Why is that? Magic is a system, not a religion. Having a witchcraft practice is a highly personal thing.

Does magic work?

Absolutely. If it didn't, I wouldn't have spent almost thirty years on it. It isn't the glitter and wind chimes that TV makes it out to be. You don't say a rhyming couplet or a magic word and have everything you ever wanted. Shocking, I know. To many, magic is focused intent that brings energy to a needed goal. For some, it could be that our focus reminds us to act in the real world to get what we want. Heck, it could be a 1 percent placebo effect, but honestly? It. Just. Works.

As a young woman at my first *real job*, I had a coworker who figured out that my car was the beater in the parking lot with the "Witches Heal" bumper sticker on it. He (a fifty-something man in another department, old enough to have outgrown this infantile behavior if he was going to) teased me relentlessly about it.

One day he ran into me at the county fair, where I was selling handmade soaps and spell oils. He said an awkward "Hi" while his wife bought my prosperity oil. I told her how to use it and bid them farewell. I saw him a week later, coming back to the fair for another bottle of oil. There's no way she could have used it all unless she dumped it out or shattered the bottle.

He sheepishly came up to me. "Can I buy another bottle of that oil?"

I looked up at him from my chair, "Certainly. I see your wife liked it. That was pretty fast for a bottle that size."

"She used it just like you said, and then won some money on the lottery the next day. I'm supposed to come to get more oil, and then go buy lottery tickets," he replied.

Guess who never gave me a hard time about magic ever again.

BASICS OF MAGIC

GROUNDING AND CENTERING

Pick up most books on magic, and you will find the phrase "ground and center." Well, is it on the ground, or in your center? A little bit of both. Centering is the practice of mentally gathering all of your scattered energies throughout your body and consciously bringing them into your center, somewhere between your belly button and your diaphragm. Grounding is the process whereby we visualize a connection to the earth, where we can draw up energies into our bodies, or send down excess energy. What does that do? It can calm an anxious mind. We can send the frenzied energy down into the earth, where it can be more efficiently utilized. We can also draw strength into our bodies when we need it.

How do we do all that?

Meditation. It isn't what we usually think when we hear the word; it isn't nothingness. This is a guided meditation, where you picture certain things happening, and it shows an effect within the body. One of the most popular is to imagine you are a tree, and that your toes are roots wiggling down into the dirt, and that your arms, hands, and fingers are branches reaching up towards the sun.

The most important part of this process is breathing. If you stop breathing, you die. So, we know that we are breathing as we move through our day. The difference lies in the intentional, mindful breath. It involves taking slow, deep breaths in through the nose and out through the mouth. This is the breath that pushes your belly out, rather than raising your chest overmuch. While we rush around our busy daily lives, we are usually in the top of our lungs breathing, using an average of 10 percent of our lung capacity.

How do you meditate?

1. Stop what you're doing.

2. Understand it is going to feel weird or awkward doing nothing for a few minutes. It's likely that your brain will tell you that you have better things to be doing right now. You don't. Those tasks will still be there in two minutes when you're done having a breath. It reduces stress; it helps clear your mind and makes it easier for your brain to access all of the creativity and information stored in your brain.

3. Breathe in slowly through your nose and out through your mouth for at least four breaths. Try to breathe out longer than your slow inhale. You might yawn; that's okay. Your body isn't used to getting this much oxygen, so it has to make sure this isn't a trick.

4. While you're breathing mindfully, don't worry about the groceries, or work, or the dishes. Instead, picture your toes wiggling down into the cool, dark earth. Connect your breath with the planet. Practice pushing energy down into the ground and bringing it back up with each breath you take. Send on the exhale, pull it in with the inhale. You can do this whether or not you can put your toes in the literal dirt. You can do this at thirty thousand feet in an airplane. The relative distance to the earth isn't what matters; it is maintaining that mental connection.

5. Once you are ready to stop, remember to keep a little energy in the center of your being for yourself. If you feel tired afterward, you didn't save enough. You can reconnect at any time and receive a little more.

Does this hurt the planet? No. It is more immense than we as individuals can comprehend. We can also send that energy to the earth whenever we choose.

Directing Energy

Once you have the practice of the ebb and flow of energy in your body down pat, it's time to move on to manipulating it. Connect with the earth, and bring some energy into your center. Now send it out to your palms. Your palms will start to tingle almost like when you get goosebumps on your arms. You can shape that energy into a ball. You can choose the size of the ball as well as the shape. You can change these through your will. Just visualize it.

When you can easily create a ball of energy between your palms, change it. Try picturing your favorite fruit. The image should be right there on the edge of your mind, along with its scent, color, and size.

This energy can be sent out into the universe as well as back into yourself. You can also push this ball of energy into a candle that can help you manifest your desires. That ball of energy can be various colors to accomplish your goals. Once you gain practice moving energy in this way, there really isn't much you can't do with it.

IN THIS BOOK

Within these pages, we'll discuss the tools needed to create potions and magical brews. You will also discover methods for making bitters and crafting your own magical vermouth, as well as techniques for brewing your own kombucha and soda flavorings from scratch, as well as everything from crafting drinks with strawberries for happiness and joy, to adding magic to your morning coffee or tea.

Your "morning ritual" can *be* a ritual. These things set the tone for our day, and if skipped, it may feel as if something is missing the rest of the day. Give yourself permission to enjoy the things you will be doing anyway.

This book is for *you*. Whether you're a barista, a bartender, or a mom who is looking to add fruits and veggies to the kids' daily routine. Whoever you are, you don't have to know anything about magic, you just need an open mind and a taste for adventure (and the occasional pun).

There are chapters on creating your own magical tea recipes, with real teas, rather than dusty, hard-to-find herbs. We will be creating the perfect cocktail for Samhain, the full moon, or just Sunday. There are tricks to designing your own signature cocktail for parties, and the kitchen chapters contain brews for health, home, and hearth, as well as for fun.

Understanding the magic of fermentation, maceration, and infusion will help us see where the magic comes from and how to live our best lives with an enchanting flair. So, come with me to discover a world of magical ingredients, disguised as the produce section of the local grocery store, as well as the magician's tools you're likely to find in the kitchen drawer. Let's make some magic together.

Remember, magic is powered by belief. And I believe in you. – Amy

What Makes It Magical?

The first topic up for discussion should be "What Is Magic?" The great thing is, you already know the answer. You've probably seen movies about magic, read faery tales, or watched them on television. These stories are full of the magic of potions, witches, and the spoken word. The magic that is less frequently spoken about, but is no less real, is the magic of being.

DEFINING MAGIC

Magic is the pitter-patter in your heart when seeing someone that catches your fancy, or the butterflies in your stomach that give you a thrill when your loved ones are near. Magic is the hair standing on end, warning you that something is about to happen. These things can be explained away with biological reasoning, but that makes them no less magical.

Fantasy author Arthur C. Clarke's Third Law states, "Any sufficiently advanced technology is indistinguishable from magic." Magic is just the name for things science doesn't understand yet. But that doesn't make them any less real. Whether we are journeying within ourselves to follow the link between the self and our environment or altering our consciousness to reach other planes, the only difference is the destination. They both deal with the realm of the possible.

Place your hand on your heart. That pulse you feel under your hand? The lub-dub of the heart's chambers working (usually) in concert is one of the hallmarks of life. Life implies biological processes, and in humans, they start with the electrical impulses. As much as we understand those biological processes and the human body, even surgeons admit they don't comprehend what makes the heart beat, or what causes this complex machine to stop working. Witches do. It's magic— plain and simple, while also being terrifyingly complex.

Art and Science

When asking a witch what magic is, one is likely to get several mixed answers. The most common is Aleister Crowley's definition, which resonates with me: "Magic is the art and science of creating change in accordance with will." That's a lot of information to take in.

Crowley didn't put "art and science" in there by mistake. The art of magic is entirely separate from the science of magic. The art of magic is the difference between a painting by one of the masters and a paint-by-numbers copy. Creating magic has art involved, in the same way painting does. Anyone can paint and have fun with it, just as anyone can recite a rhyming couplet. (Yes, anyone. Signed languages have as much art and poetry as any spoken word.) What makes the difference between a rhyming couplet and magic is the spirit of the person reciting them.

I've been asked in an untold number of interviews if the spells cast in popular witchcraft media like *Charmed* are real. That's a double-edged sword. Are they magic? Not yet, no. But they could be soon. Magic requires thought and intention, among other things. Saying the words isn't enough; we have to put thought and intent into them.

When my niece E. came to me, sometime around eight years old, asking if Santa Claus was real, "Yes" was my immediate response. No, I wasn't humoring her. I promised I'd always be honest with her, and I was. There is a concept known in magical circles as an *egregor* (pronounced *E-gr'g-Or*). An egregor is a thoughtform, a thoughtform that has been thought of by so many people, for so many years, in such a varied population, that it becomes its own autonomous entity. The idea is that Santa has been thought of for long enough that he became a true spirit of Christmas. He may not occupy a physical place on our plane, but he exists in spirit.

Magical spells that exist in popular culture could be used in spells by witches, but just because it was on television, doesn't make it real. Witches aren't battling demons weekly, and you won't find the potions from the world of *Charmed* within these pages. The only thing real in pop culture magic is usually the dry ice.

Magic should make you feel something. You should feel something before you start the spell, while creating it, and after you have finished the spell. If there is no feeling attached, there can be no magic. I'm not suggesting you have to experience an extreme passion to work practical magic, but there needs to be some feeling to tap into. If you don't care enough about the issue, it's like a chocolate bunny in the spring: it looks good, but it's hollow. We can be passionate about a subject without being hysterical.

SCIENCE AND MAGIC

Some feel that science and magic are antithetical, but scientists make great witches. In a way, both witches and scientists use the Scientific Method. For those of you who are a little rusty, the Scientific Method is a (generally) agreed-upon set of procedures in investigating anything related to science.

7 STEPS OF THE SCIENTIFIC METHOD

Step 1—Pose your question.
This is the thing that you want to know. The problem or the question you want to answer. "Does gravity work?"

Step 2—Design and conduct research.
"Step 1: I will drop something."

Step 3—Form your hypothesis.
"I think it will fall."

Step 4—Experiment, testing the hypothesis.
Drop several things; record observations.

Step 5—Make observations based on the data you collect during the experiments.
"Everything that was dropped eventually wound up on the floor. Different rates of descent, but they all landed."

Step 6—Use your results to form your conclusion.
Does your experiment support your hypothesis? Conclusion: "I'm pretty sure gravity works."

Step 7—Communicate with others in the field and out.
Present/share your findings. Attempt to replicate your results. Tell peers you think gravity works; keep dropping things and recording notes.

7 STEPS OF THE WITCHCRAFT METHOD

Step 1—State the need.
This could be a spell, or a small part in a more extensive ritual incorporating many elements of ritual, including candles, quarter calls, and the like. "Money" is okay, but better results are attained from a more specific intention. "I need money for a new car." Whenever possible, state the need in the positive, rather than negative. "I don't have money for a new car" isn't as magically effective as "I need money for a new car." The theory is that our minds don't grasp the negative words when doing magic so that it can impact the working. The best wording, however, is "I have money for a new car." You're acting as though the goal has already been attained. It leaves room in the universe to provide what you need, or something better.

Step 2—Conduct research.

You'll need correspondences for the stated need, "plants associated with prosperity" or "stones for money" and the like. Write them all out first, then narrow the focus from there. The reason for this method is two-fold: it makes it easier to see patterns, and it has been proven that we retain more information when it is handwritten, rather than typed. (Hint: Use blue ink for a memory boost; it is different from the black typeface so it stands out in our mind for easier recall.)

Step 3—Write the spell/ritual.

First, decide how complicated the working should be. Is this a simple issue with a simple solution, like a candle spell? Or is this a complicated matter that requires an in-depth ritual to build the power needed?

Step 4—Do the thing.

The minute you decide a spell needs to happen, in Step 1, the clock starts ticking. Every moment you spend researching materials, choosing the working, shopping for materials required is energy that goes toward the intended outcome: the more power, the more likely the intended result.

Step 5—Make observations.

The data you collect during and after the spell gets recorded in your Book of Shadows, just like a scientist would. "A week later, I won the office birthday pool for Sally's new baby," or "thirteen days later, still no results." Even if the spell doesn't work, it can be illuminating to look at the potential reasons why. Perhaps you look at the time the working started and find out the moon was void of course, or between signs. That can muddy the magical waters, so try not to do workings when the moon is between signs. Your magical calendar or ephemeris might have it marked as "Moon v/c 6:04 p.m."

Step 6— Use your results to form your conclusion.

If your intention came to pass the way it was designed, great! I'm happy for you. If it didn't, many factors could have contributed to the failure of the ritual. Before you declare it null, wait for at least a full lunar cycle, twenty-eight days, for the intention to come to pass. You don't want to decide a working failed before it has a chance to work.

The reasons for failure can include:

» **Doubt**—It's the killer of all magic. The fastest way to make sure your magic won't come to pass is to doubt that it will. The power comes from you, not the candles, incense, or chants. So if you think you don't have the oomph needed, don't doubt, work it out.

» **Lack of power**—When casting your intention, putting your spell out into the ether, you have to feel it in your bones. If it feels like you are reciting your phone number for a telemarketer, you are not going to have the desired results. Sound off like you mean it. Speaking of meaning it, stop and take stock to make sure this is something you really want. It could be that the reason a workable amount of energy cannot be raised is that it isn't a sincere desire.

» **Patience**—It takes time for magic to work. Sometimes it happens that your working works right away, but that happens less often than you might think, and frequently after a lot of practice. Magic is a skill, no matter how many witches you see in movies and television discovering they are magical. Within two minutes, they know everything about spells and are calling everyone *mundanes*. (By the way, that's not a thing. As much as we enjoy our witchy friends, community, and festivals, there is no mundane world. We get one world; take your magic with you.) Take a deep breath and know your intention is working.

» **Shoddy scholarship**—There is a reason that witches and even faerie tale wizards are associated with books. Knowledge is power, and without the know-how, your magic isn't going to get any wind in its sails. Take the time to do the research needed to feel supported and fulfilled in your magical endeavors; after all, you are building your magical intent and your brain.

» **Lack of focus**—If your magic doesn't have a specific outcome, it scatters your attention, and therefore your intention. If your original plan is "Money for a new car" and mid spell you start thinking how nice it would be to have some new clothes, but then you'd "have to work more hours, to pay for the clothes, and I really should get a new job, I'm miserable here, and my boss is a jerk, and . . . " Do you see how that can take the fire out of the spell? Concentrate while you are working and find a friend to vent to later. The same goes for trying to cast a spell in a house full of people, or in a messy room. All of these things can scatter your focus.

» **Too many cooks in the kitchen**—I'll be the first to tell you that working magic with friends and loved ones is fun. It can bring people closer together and is an excellent way to bond. (PS: No matter how cool sex magic sounds, do not engage with a partner who is unaware that this is what you're doing—consent is essential.) That aside, bringing a friend, loved one, or partner into your magical practice should be done carefully if at all. The idea of a coven sounds scintillating and neat. However, having a new practitioner, who may or may not have a clear picture of what to do or how to do it, can break down the building energy. Not to mention, if your spell is for a new car, and your BFF thinks you need a sensible older model and to pay down your debt, it can break down the momentum you were gaining doing all the research. If you want to practice with magical friends, keep it simple and make sure everyone is on the same page.

» **Volatile emotions**—If you're too upset to drive, or crying too hard to talk, those emotions can hinder your magical practice. I'm not talking about mental health either; telling people they have to be 100 percent mentally healthy before someone will love them is harmful and ableist. I'm saying giving yourself time to collect your thoughts and feelings, wipe the tears away, and ground yourself, makes for a more focused intent. Also, trying to work magic when emotional can lead us to overextend our energy and feel drained and unfocused later. By properly grounding before spell work, we ensure that we are connected to the earth and a well of energy.

Step 7—Communicate. Present/share your results. Replicate.
When communicating the results of a spell, await the full results, or 28 days before declaring it a failure. Spell work takes time.

The Witches' Pyramid says: "To Know, To Will, To Dare, To Keep Silent." Exclaiming to your circle of friends you've completed the "coolest spell ever" isn't the best idea. It can introduce doubt into the spell from outsiders, from yourself if they aren't 100 percent supportive, or from magical practitioner friends who don't see the outcome the same way you do. So, wait a bit before declaring you're the best witch in all of history, okay?

Unintended complications from magic can happen. For example, you needed cash, but after the money came in, an unexpected bill came up.

Perhaps in addition to keeping magical records, you want to start an online journal, a blog, or even a channel to speak to other witches about your experiences. Being a magical practitioner can feel lonely if you don't know anyone. If you feel that way, I guarantee there are thousands of others like you who feel isolated and could benefit from your experiences.

MAKING MAGIC

Unfortunately, all of this nebulous talk of magic doesn't really shine a light on how magic gets made. There is a disconnect between the brain and the heart when it comes to making magic happen. It comes from watching magic on TV and from reading about it in books. New witches see fictional characters reciting "magic words" and bam! There are some sparkly special effects to tell us magic has happened and something amazing results. In real life, we don't get the light cues or the faint chime to let us know our spell was effective. What this televised visual method leaves out is the hair-raising knowing that comes with our magic. The tingle in your palms that says the energy was raised. You can have all of the aesthetics right and still not raise any energy. *Ritual theater* (the costumes, masks, robes, and the like) will only get you so far.

A NOTE ON CURSES, HEXES, AND JINXES

In this age of "love and light," it is important to remind readers that any living thing exposed to light, and only light, all day and all night, will shrivel and die. Living things need rest. Nature needs balance. Without light, there is no darkness. Plant a seed; it's in the dark.

Darkness does not mean badness. This idea comes from a racist heritage and needs to be corrected. White does not equal good. Black does not equal bad. Telling people that standing up for themselves and refusing to accept abuse makes them wrong enables abuse. No one deserves to be abused. Ever. If magic is agency, then hexes or bane work is the available recourse for wrongs done. It is not our job to heal our abusers. PS: Karma doesn't apply here either. Karma is a concept that belongs to Buddhism and Hinduism and applies across lifetimes, for the next lifetime. Karma has nothing to do with being cut off in traffic or even spell casting.

The Rule of Three that is often lauded as the be-all/end-all is mostly misunderstood. It is not a universal law, as it applies mainly to Wiccans and not even all Wiccans. The Rule of Three isn't some magical multiplication table designed to make us feel bad or to punish wrongdoers. If that were the case, there would be fewer wrongdoers and a lot more abusers in prison. What this principle refers to is the effect our magic has on our 1) mind, 2) body, and 3) spirit. What this means is that if you feel wrong about a spell you've cast, that guilt will weigh on your conscience, you might have stomach cramps or some other physical sign, and you'll feel cruddy about yourself. If you're feeling guilty, you can remediate the spell you've done as best you can. It does not mean three bad things are going to happen to you because you're a terrible person. If you aren't feeling guilty, none of those things happen.

Poet Victor Anderson, co-founder of the Feri witchcraft tradition, once said, "White magic is poetry; black magic is anything that actually works." While I've already explained that this is a false dichotomy and hurtful to people of color, it is worth stating that magic that works affects, by definition. Good and evil are so subjective. Doing a job spell to get work because I've been out of work is good, right? I'll be able to pay my bills and contribute financially. But if you get that job, someone, or several someones who also have costs, didn't get it. You want to ease the suffering of a friend with terminal cancer, but prolonging their suffering is cruel. Cursing child molesters so they are caught and incarcerated means that they can't harm children while locked away. These are all things we need to think about when discussing our magical intent.

Good vibes are a nice thought, but intention doesn't always count as much as we think it should. The most popular metaphor for this is dropping a plate on the floor and having it shatter. Apologizing to the plate isn't going to magically repair the damage done. The plate isn't showered in a rain of glitter that makes it all better, the way TV magic makes it seem. Everyone messes up sometimes. Words hurt. Own up to it and apologize with feeling and conviction. The hardest part of apologizing is knowing that no one is obligated to forgive us for wrongdoing. That's scary because it makes us vulnerable, but that doesn't mean we don't owe it to ourselves and others to be the best person we can be, whether or not someone is there to absolve you of your guilt.

MAKING OUR DRINKS INTO POTIONS

Picture yourself at a concert, something loud and fun, or a sporting event where the stands are packed, and the crowd is one living organism. Everyone is stomping their feet and clapping their hands. The energy of that stadium can be used for magic. That energy is what gets spells going. There are all sorts of methods for raising energy, from singing and dancing to clapping, drumming, and laughing. The most important part is what to do with the energy once it has been raised. In a coven setting, the entire group raises the energy, and the high priestess is responsible for directing the symphony of all the coven members and sending the energy where it needs to go. When you're a solitary practitioner, all of that falls to you. But that's okay. The circle-casting lesson is another place, and another time. For our purposes, raising the energy and directing it into the beverages we are making, and thus making them a potion, is where we need to be.

Now let's try a different visual. Picture yourself in a moonlit grotto. You're carrying a chalice as you step from the trees and into the clearing. The moonlight is so bright, you can see clearly. As you walk toward the center of the clearing, you see the moon is shining onto a lake. You step toward the ancient waters and see cool, clear, spring-fed water filling the lake. Take a bit of the water into the chalice for yourself. Raise it to the moon and allow the rays to reach into the depths of the water. Feel the heartbeat of the earth. Feel the energy of the earth rise through your feet, calves, legs, hips, belly, up through your arms, and into the glass. Feel where the earth and the moon meet in the palms of your hands. See the energy pour out the top of the glass as you raise it to your lips and drink it all. That wasn't water. It was a potion to bring life to your magic. Once the water became infused with the energy of the moon and of the earth, it became that potion.

We worked with water for a few reasons:

» It's hypoallergenic.

» It demonstrates that any potable beverage can be magical.

» Water can be found in many places.

Now try it again with the chalice and no water, and remind yourself that the magic is within you, and not the water. Now do the ritual with no chalice and no water. Simply see the water, see the cup in your mind's eye, and feel the power that is raised each time and how they may or may not feel different. Now you can charge your water daily before you drink it, to draw anything you desire.

STEPS FOR MAKING MAGIC WITH POTIONS

Step 1—Think of your desired goal.
You've got to have a clear picture of the end result before you start.

Step 2—Create a drink of choice.
Pour a cup of cola. "But that's not magical," you protest. Sure, it is. Cola derives its name from the kola nut, the fruit of the kola tree. It's what gives modern-day cola drinks a good bit of their caffeine! So, stimulants make things *go*. Picture your favorite five-year-olds, all sugared up on soda. They're going places; we're just along for the ride. Things that make people go can make our magic go. So, pour that soda.

Step 3—Raise energy.
Tell a joke. Sing a song. Dance. Just get that energy moving. Once it has been sufficiently raised, direct all the power into the soda cup.

Step 4—Drink!
You can drink it fast or slow. Is it a hot day, or do you want to relax with a cup of tea and think about your intention while you sip slowly? The energy is there, waiting.

Tools of
the (Brew) Craft

When is a spoon not a spoon?
When it's a wand! This chapter talks about the everyday implements we encounter when creating our brews and potions, and how they can align with a magical mindset. Before we can delve into the ritual use of our bar tools, we should first examine the traditional witch's tools.

WAND-MUDDLER

The extension of the wand is the *stang*. The stang is a staff that has a forked end. It can be used to cast or mark a circle, as well as to direct energy. Traditionally wands are made of wood and run the length of the witch's inner elbow to the tip of the middle finger. As each witch is a different height, it leads to lots of variation in the wand. Each wood also confers a different magical association. Wands are used to invoke elementals, spirits *allergic* to iron. It is possible, and sometimes encouraged, to have more than one, but it is not necessary to have tools, and some traditions restrict owning tools until one has been initiated. That may sound severe, but it helps witches develop a natural appreciation for their tools, without relying on them for work. Remember, you are the magic.

MUDDLER

Wooden muddlers are used for crushing ingredients against the bottom of a glass to release their flavors and mix them. Famously used to crush mint for the perfect mojito (from the Spanish word *mojado,* meaning wet), this tool is known for expressing citrus, so both the juice from the fruit and oil from the rind make it into the drink. This gives the drink a more sustainable flavor; as the ice melts, the oil from the peel still stands out. If you don't have a muddler on hand, you can use the handle end of a rolling pin, or the backside of a spoon. If you want the flavor of a chosen greenery, but don't want to impart the color of the chlorophyll, simply slap the herbs on a hard surface a few times, and add them to the drink. They will be fragrant without turning your drink green.

MAGICAL USES

Athames (*ATH-amay,* a witch's double-edged knife) have been used to direct will and invocation, but wands do that as well. The difference? The entities that are offended by iron—elementals and the like—can be invoked with the wooden wand instead. Invocation is a summoning of the gods, ancestors, elementals, and others for offerings, or to request aid or communication.

Mojito Magic Spell

According to legend, the mojito was invented during the days of slavery, when the enslaved sought to elicit kinder behavior from their slave masters, sugarcane plantation owners. Think of it as a drinkable Bend Over Oil (a magical formula used to make bosses kinder and more compliant to the users' aims or goals). The magical origins of the mojito may be contested, but the magic of these ingredients isn't. Peppermint has a list of magical attributes longer than my arm, and adding the raw power of your favorite rum can't hurt.

Tools

» Highball glass

» Pub glass or pint glass

Ingredients

» Enough ice to chill a glass

» 1 oz. light rum

» 9 mint leaves

» 1 tbsp. superfine sugar (also called caster sugar or baker's sugar)—powdered sugar will remain lumpy, and table sugar won't dissolve readily. If you don't have superfine sugar, you can pulse table sugar in a food processor, or make simple syrup—see Chapter 8 for techniques.

» 1 lime cut into pieces, plus extra for garnish

» 3 oz. club soda

Add half the ice usually used into the highball glass and let chill. We'll add more in a moment.

Close your eyes and connect with the earth. Envision a pale blue thread of peace leaving your heels and burying itself deep within the planet, allowing you to draw up the energies you need from therein.

Muddle the mint leaves in the bottom of an empty pub glass.

Envision the intention you are empowering (clarity, healing, prosperity, banishing) and direct energy you draw up from the earth and send it down through the muddler and into those mint leaves to release their highest potential.

Add the tablespoon of superfine sugar to the muddled mint. This will dissolve quickly. Muddle mint and sugar to incorporate. Continue envisioning your outcome while sending energy into the muddler.

Toss the cut lime pieces into the cup and muddle until the sugar is dissolved.

Add the rum to the muddle and give it a few more swishes before pouring into the chilled highball glass. Top with 3 oz. club soda. Garnish with lime.

Sober Substitution: Hold the mint as a bunch by the end, and slap it on the table three times. This will release the flavor of the mint without turning your drink green. Place into the glass. Add the superfine sugar to the glass and squeeze the lime wedges into the glass. Feel free to add some lime zest as well! Give the mix a good stir while sending the blue light into your drink, and top with club soda while imagining the intended outcome.

Peppermint is associated with action, alertness, antidepressant, awakening, and so many other uses. For a full list, please see *Blackthorn's Botanical Magic.*

We can invoke a treasure trove of traits by partnering with peppermint. We can ally with peppermint to establish good study habits at the beginning of a project or semester. We can awaken our awareness of our psychic senses and banish any blocks to our creative expression. You can make a cup of mint tea and empower it with your intention of choice; add a little sugar for a free jolt of energy and a magical reminder that life can be sweet if we allow the universe to bring us what we need most.

CHALICE—GLASSWARE AND SPOONS

The extension of the chalice is the cauldron. I'm sure you've seen cauldrons in Halloween cartoons and spooky movies. But rather than bubbling vats of dry ice and water, they are much more likely to be used for burning candles and incense in a fireproof container. Often the chalice is made of metal, but the construction is less important than the feeling of the sacred when you see it. If that means that your chalice cost fifty cents at a secondhand shop, great. If that means that you carved your chalice from wood, that's lovely. If you found the perfect cup in a new age catalog, or at the renaissance fair, that is also perfect. The job of the chalice is to a) hold beverages, and b) in traditional witchcraft illustrate the Great Rite in token. The athame is inserted into the chalice filled with a drink as a symbolic union of man and woman, and the drink is therefore blessed. Then the chalice is passed (or carried) around. So, whether you pick something large enough for a group, or choose a biodegradable paper cup, go with the one that feels right.

GLASSWARE

Glasses are the everyday equivalent to the altar's chalice. The chalice is the cup of transformation. The ancient world saw the womb as the liminal space that it is. The womb can produce offspring; the ancients did not understand at first the correlation between sex and procreation. Associations of cups with the womb of the goddess are found from the Neolithic era to Holy Grail mythos and early modern era witchcraft books from the 1950s. But this "sword equals penis" and "chalice equals womb" subterfuge is so limited. It cuts out our enbie friends, nonbinary, genderfluid, and gender nonconforming witches. One can quickly look to the ancient gods and see that, even among the divine, gender is a spectrum, and this is not a new idea.

BEER MUG

This old standby, with its heavy bottom and thick handle, usually holds sixteen ounces of fluid. This glass is great for thinking. Pour anything in there, beer, soda, even lemonade. This dense, dependable glass is sturdy enough to be grounding while you ponder a problem or examine the origins of the universe. It's like a weighted blanket for your hand.

BRANDY SNIFTER

This small and round glass is an excellent five-ounce friend; it sits well in the palm and lends itself to artful swirling while musing over puzzles.

Rather than the ice-cold lemonade of the beer mug, a snifter is well suited for aromatic lavender lemonade, as well as Cognac and other liqueurs. If you think with your hands, use all the air of the snifter to draw you in.

CHAMPAGNE SAUCER, OR COUP

Seen mostly at weddings, this shallow relative of the champagne flute isn't keen on keeping the signature bubbles coming. It's better suited to delicate and aromatic cocktails like the Corpse Reviver. This popular drink from the 1920s and '30s deserves its reputation for resurrecting the dead. With absinthe, gin, and more on board, it's less hair of the dog, and more the *whole* dog.

Corpse Reviver
(for protection, purification, and transcendence)

Tools

- » Champagne saucer
- » Cocktail shaker
- » Optional: Hawthorne strainer

Ingredients

- » 1 oz. Cointreau (abundance, antidepressant, affection)
- » 1 oz. lemon juice (calming, clarity, blessing)
- » 1 oz. Lillet Blanc (refreshing, balancing, connection)
- » 1 oz. gin (protection of the mind, purification, aura cleansing)
- » A splash of absinthe (transcendence, other realms)

Fill the champagne saucer with ice to chill the glass.
Add all liquors into the cocktail shaker.

Fill the shaker with ice and cap. See yourself whole, surrounded by brilliant light, and protected from outside harm. Let the picture become more apparent as you shake.

Shake until frost appears on the metal of the cocktail shaker.

Dump the ice out of the glass.

Fill the glass using the shaker's pour spout or a Hawthorne strainer.

Garnish with a cherry and drink, knowing you'll be just fine.

Death in the Afternoon
(for trance, other realms, parting the veil)

Ernest Hemingway is credited with creating this sublime cocktail and reportedly drank way too many of them. Maybe he was trying to rend the veil himself.

Tools

» Champagne saucer

Ingredients

» 4½ oz. champagne or sparkling wine (broadcast your magic to the universe, fertility—of body or wallet, all-purpose magical boost)

» 1½ oz. absinthe (meditation, astral travel, trance work)

Ground and center.

Pour the absinthe into the glass and see your essence slipping into the glass.

Top with champagne for a delightful emerald glow. Broadcast your astral self into the heavens whilst sipping. I'll admit, I've used Moscato for this, as I have a sweet tooth.

TULIP GLASS

This is the quintessential champagne flute. It is tall, slender, and allows the champagne or sparkling wine to retain its effervescent nature and allows the flavors of the wine to bloom on the tongue.

Mimosa Marvel Spell

As champagne is made from grapes, this spell is the perfect vehicle to announce your intent to the world! No cheating on this one; skip the bottled orange juices in the refrigerator section and grab a gorgeous, ripe orange from the produce section. Word around the cauldron is that this decadent brunch staple was invented at the Ritz in Paris in the 1920s.

Tools

> » Champagne flute

Ingredients

> » 5 oz. chilled champagne (broadcast your intent to the universe)
>
> » 2½ oz. orange juice—juice half an orange (abundance, action, acceptance, emotional clarity)
>
> » ½ oz. Cointreau (authority, creativity, fortune)

Pour the Cointreau into the flute and top with orange juice.
Fill the champagne flute with champagne.
Give a little stir (clockwise while seeing yourself successful).

Sober Substitution: Juice the orange, fill the glass the rest of the way with sparkling cider (apples are associated with love, fertility, and emotional support), and express the orange peel over the top of the flute for an orangey bite.

Ginger Rogers Passion Spell

You know, Ginger Rogers did everything Fred Astaire did, except backward and in heels. When you've found your passion, you want to empower your hobbies, or want inspiration to follow your dreams, try this.

Tools

- » Cocktail shaker
- » Champagne flute

Ingredients

- » 5 oz. of chilled champagne (fertility, making a statement before the gods)
- » 1 oz. bourbon (the magic of growth and transformation)
- » 1 oz. pineapple juice (happiness, joy, fulfillment)
- » 3 ginger coins—slice ginger thinly through the center "short ways" so the pieces come out looking like coins (energizing, luck, improvement, passion, protection)
- » Ice

Place bourbon, ginger, and pineapple juice in a cocktail shaker with ice.

Shake vigorously until frost forms on the metal of the shaker. Shaking the cocktail shaker is charging your potion with intent. The more you shake, and the more vigorously you shake, the more energy you're raising for those dreams!

When it feels like your arms can't swing anymore, push all the power you've built into the cocktail shaker. Breathe out.

Strain into a chilled champagne flute and top with champagne. Ground and center again while sipping this delight and see yourself in passionate love with the life you'll be living.

Sober Substitution: Replace the bourbon with ginger ale and the champagne with sparkling cider. Shake pineapple juice, ginger, and ice in a shaker. Strain into a champagne flute. Add ginger ale and sparkling cider.

MARTINI GLASS

 This is the traditional cocktail glass (terms used interchangeably) famously used for the Bond, James Bond of drinks, the martini. It can handle upwards of six ounces of liquid in the standard and ten ounces in the larger glass.

The Lady Godiva Gratitude Spell

This sweet and chocolaty dessert cocktail is the living embodiment of the more beautiful things in life. Chocolate is undoubtedly on the list of things most fine. This working is gratitude in a glass, and through our thanks, we make room for more of the same.

Lady Godiva rode nude through Coventry or at least according to the stories originating in the 13th century. As the story goes, the lord's taxes were hurting the people badly. Lady Godiva (*Godgyfu* in old English, God's Gift in modern English) kept imploring her husband to lower taxes so that their people could live. First, he tried to threaten her station: "We need money to pay for the fancy clothes you wear." She denied it. Thinking to outsmart her, he agreed to lower the taxes if she would ride naked through the town square. She agreed. Upon seeing she meant it, the jealous lord proclaimed that no one should see the lady riding nude through the town. No one, save one tailor named Tom, spied on the woman as she passed, clothed only in her long hair. (That's where we get the expression Peeping Tom.)

First, make a list of things you are thankful for in your life. Dig out parchment paper and fancy pens if you've got them. Really illustrate the things that you are happy for and make you proud. Have you earned your prestige in a particular area? Have you reached or surpassed a goal? Did you do something you were told you wouldn't be able to accomplish? Write it all out.

On a separate piece of paper list the things you want to bring into your life now that you have your project, goal, or achievement.

Tools

» Cocktail shaker

» Cocktail glass

Ingredients

» 1½ oz. heavy whipping cream (cleansing, healing, protection)

» 1 oz. vodka (protection, money, luck, healing, public image)

» ½ oz. crème de cacao—Godiva's chocolate liqueur is fitting, but not required (prosperity, fertility, offering to gods, love, lust)

» 1 tsp. sugar syrup (reminder of the sweetness of life)

Place all ingredients into a cocktail shaker and add ice.

Shake vigorously until frost forms on the shaker. See everything on the second list coming to pass just as the things you're already thankful for having.

Strain into a cocktail glass.

Drink while giving your acceptance speech to The Academy for your particular level of awesome.

Burn both lists and release your intention.

Sober Substitution: Make hot chocolate from scratch. The heat of the stove empowers the magic in the way that shaking the cocktail shaker does. The spell is released when you take the first sip.

Tools

- » Saucepan
- » Whisk

Ingredients

- » Old-fashioned hot chocolate
- » 4 cups milk (cleansing, healing, protection)
- » ½ cup sugar (remind of the sweetness of life)
- » $^1/_3$ cup hot water
- » ¼ cup cocoa powder (prosperity, fertility, offering to gods, love, lust)
- » 1 tsp. vanilla extract (calm, peace, love, passion)
- » $^1/_8$ tsp. salt (purification)

Place salt, cocoa, and sugar in a saucepan. Add hot water.

Turn the heat to medium and stir constantly. Boil for 2 minutes and reduce heat.

Gently add milk (splashes can burn). Continue stirring until hot, but don't scald the milk, or you'll have to start over. Scalded milk is awful.

Whisk in vanilla. Makes four 9 oz. servings.

SPOONS

Spoons are associated with cups, chalices, and cauldrons due to their shape, which is reminiscent of their serving sisters.

ABSINTHE SPOON

A decorative slotted spoon (frequently crimped along the handle to rest securely on the rim of a glass), this spoon holds sugar cubes over the bitter elixir of your choice (typically absinthe) so that water can be dripped over the sugar and into the glass. Organic sugar cubes dissolve more quickly and are best for traditional absinthe preparation. The dissolved sugar sweetens bitter drinks and makes them a little more palatable. It's essential that absinthe spoons are made of metal, as, depending on rituals and preparations, fire may be involved. Because it is used for fire as well as water, the absinthe spoon is a tool of liminality, and it exists between two worlds.

Magical uses: Transformation. This spoon often has a flat, paddle-shaped area in the handle to hold a sugar cube and is highly decorative. Think of the absinthe spoon as the transformational tool, part knife-part spoon. It can cut ties after a painful separation, whether friendships or romantic partnerships. It can be used to break bad habits, when, as a phoenix, you rise from the ashes.

Phoenix Rising Spell

Take a sugar cube (use an old-fashioned, white sugar one for this), and name it with a bad habit you want to break, or a personality trait you'd like to get rid of. Dip it into high-proof absinthe—less than 100 proof won't do it. Place the absinthe spoon over the glass and set the cube on the spoon. Carefully light the cube and watch that old you go up in flames. As the alcohol burns off, it will caramelize the sugar. Carefully drop the cube off the spoon and into the drink. Add *ice cold* water to the glass. It will put out the fire and produce the hazy green glow for which absinthe is renowned. Drink a toast to the new you! Drink responsibly. Remember, absinthe isn't called the Green Fairy for nothing!

> **Sober Substitution:** This may be accomplished by using a 97 percent isopropyl alcohol to light the sugar cube. Then wash the caramelized sugar down the drain. *Never* ingest isopropyl (rubbing) alcohol. Optional: make a soda from Chapter 8, and toast your new life.

BAR SPOON

This long-legged cousin to the tablespoon is designed to make stirring drinks in tall glasses a breeze. The handle is often spiraled to make the drink less likely to splash when mixed—similar to the spoons used to blend milkshakes, where that spiral is part of the mixing mechanism.

Magical uses: The wand shape makes this capable of directing your will, while the bowl shape of the spoon is useful for softening the truth, for the truth is often a bitter pill to swallow. It doesn't hurt to add a little sweetness to the mix.

Hard to Handle Spell

Have you ever had to tell a friend something painful or potentially hurtful? Do you need to set a boundary but don't want to lose a friendship? Want to broach the subject, but are fearful the words may come out wrong? Choose the ingredient that best suits your intention and make a syrup using your bar spoon to send your purpose into the syrup. (See the syrup section in Chapter 8 if you need help!)

- » Anise—personal growth

- » Black Pepper—courage (Black pepper makes sweet things taste sweeter, great on strawberries)

- » Cardamom—confidence

- » Ginger—love, passion

- » Lavender—truth

- » Mandarin—clarity

- » Orange—acceptance

Use the syrup of choice when you sit down with your friend to have that heart-to-heart over tea. If they are long distance, make yourself some tea for courage or confidence before picking up the phone. Even if it's frightening, try to have the conversation over the phone rather than text or instant message, as it can be hard to interpret tone from the written word, especially under duress.

ATHAME—KNIVES, STRIPPERS, AND ZESTERS

The extension of the athame (pronounced *ATH-a-may* or a-*THAM-ay*) is the sword. This (traditionally black-handled) double-edged blade represents our will. I say *will* as though it should be in capital letters because it is a divine expression of our directive. The intention is what animates us, drives us to achieve new goals, and it is the will that sparks our magical practice. The standard athame is a four-inch blade with two cutting edges because our will can cut more than one way.

Contrary to what the horror movie genre will have you believe, athames are used to direct energy, and not for cutting.

The boline (white-handled knife) is used for mundane tasks of cutting herbs, rope, candles, and the like. They are often a double-edged knife that has a sickle-shaped blade.

The athame illustrates the directing of energy most clearly when used to cast a circle. Visually, the athame is cutting a circle in the air. Energetically, the athame is cutting a hole in the universe, outside of time and space. This is one of the reasons it is frequently taboo to have clocks and watches inside of the ritual space. The ritual should be the focus, not the outside world.

KNIVES

Knives are related to the athame, which has two edges; these bar tools have only one.

PARING KNIFE

This small, easy-to-handle kitchen essential can handle anything from opening ingredient packages to slicing your citrus garnish.

Magical uses: Cutting ties with people, places, and things; energetic as well as mundane cuts; drawing a line in the sand, proverbial and otherwise. Though it has a point, I don't recommend it for carving purposes. It's too unwieldy and has a high potential for cutting oneself. Candle scribes make a much better tool for that. If you don't have a witchy shop nearby, visit the local hardware store. They'll have a large selection of nails that can act as a candle scribe more safely than something with an edge.

Peaceful Parting Spell

Knives are useful for directing our will, our true intent, but even better? They cut things. When it is time to end a partnership, business, friendship, or romantic entanglement, you can cut the cords binding you with ease.

For this spell (best started on the full moon or a Friday), figural candles are best, but the chime candles you find in any new age or witchy shop will work. Name one candle with your name and one with the other person's name; the candles' color should be something that reflects you and the other person. If using figure candles, write the name of each person on the bottom of the candle under the feet. They'll burn last and keep the impression the longest.

Take cotton cord (the kind used to tie poultry before cooking works best) and knot one end around your candle and the other end around theirs. Wind until they meet at the center of the string. Allow the candles to sit together, tied up for three minutes, three hours, or three days. Threes are terrifically magical, and as the moon changes signs every two and a half days, you know the moon will be in a different sign if you wait the three days. The longer they stay tied together, the better, but sometimes we don't have the luxury of waiting.

When it's time to proceed, start winding the string around their candle, taking up the slack from your candle. When you reach *your* feet, take up the paring knife and cut the cord away. Set your candle on the fireproof surface—an old cookie sheet will work just fine. Take up the end of the string you've just cut from your candle's feet. Start to tie knots in it, working your way to their candle. See the road between you closed. That person has no power over you. You are taking your power back with each knot.

> *"By knot of one, this spell has begun.*
> *By knot of two, you pay your dues.*
> *By knot of three, I am free.*
> *By knot of four, no more tears, I pour.*
> *By knot of five, I feel alive.*
> *By knot of six, no one falls for your tricks.*
> *By knot of seven, myself, I've forgiven.*
> *By knot of eight, you won't be late.*
> *By knot of nine, I'm feeling fine.*
> *By knot of ten, there's no "remember when?"*
> *By knot of eleven, no hell or heaven.*
> *By knot of twelve, this spell I salve."*

Cut the twine with the paring knife from the second figure's feet and light both candles, back to back. As they burn (if safe to do so), move the candles further apart on the tray until they're as far away as they can get and still be fire-safe. Dispose of the candle remains in a paper bag, at a busy 24-hour big box store's trash can. You can be sure it won't be there the next time you come back.

CITRUS STRIPPER

This wand-like tool makes short work of citrus garnishes, without the potential for broken peels or broken skin that a paring knife could do. The curved blade makes a uniform quarter-inch-wide cut, with safety guides to prevent adding any unintentional ingredients, like bits of you. If you don't have one handy, reach for a vegetable peeler before the paring knife as it's a safer choice. Both the citrus stripper and the veggie peeler make excellent tools for working with ginger or making chocolate shavings for garnishes.

> *Hint: if you're peeling the ginger, you don't need either of these, as you can peel ginger with a spoon and keep more of that spicy heat for yourself.*

Magical uses: Citruses are associated with protection, healing, joy, and the sun. Also used for removing the *rot* of a situation and banishing work. Citrus strippers have such a precise groove to them that you can use them to remove anything that no longer serves.

Gotta Go Spell

Tools

>> Pen

>> Citrus stripper or peeler

Ingredients

>> 1 orange

A friend starts to change and is no longer welcome in the friends' group? Poly partner picking fights? Write their name on an orange with a pen (orange's magic includes authority, action, ambition, and focus) and then carve all traces of the name from the orange. Start with the first letter of their name, going in order, while seeing their influence on your lives coming to an end. Throw the peel outside somewhere off your property (in a planter, in the trash, or under a bush for the nutrients) before peeling the rest of the orange and eating it, thinking about good times ahead. Feel free to get everyone impacted by this person's wrongdoing involved. If they aren't magical practitioners, offer to share sections of the orange with them to remind them of acceptance, emotional clarity on the issue, or attraction for a new person in the group (either platonic or romantic).

ZESTER

This cutting tool is used to obtain the peel from a citrus fruit, as the oils that are present in the peel are often trapped until the peel is pierced or scratched. Those flavors are brighter and more sustainable than the juice itself. A zester can release a more brilliant flavor and has a shallower cutting depth than its citrus stripper counterpart. For our purposes here, a zester corresponds to the athame, as it releases the will or soul of the fruit in the peel. The volatile oils contained in the peel are the concentrated essence of the orange. Find the full list of associations for oranges and other citrus in Chapter 5.

The Orange Enterprise Spell

Orange is associated with assisting business owners, ambition, and action as well as the emotional clarity and focus to step boldly into our power. Allow the humble orange to remind you how powerful you and your dreams are.

Tools

- » Zester
- » Heavy-bottomed glass
- » Muddler
- » Cocktail shaker

- » Large brandy snifter
- » Hawthorne strainer

See Tool Substitutions at end of recipe for more information.

Ingredients

- » 1 orange (confidence, action, ability, focus)
- » 2 oz. orange vodka (protection, business assistance, ambition, emotional clarity)
- » 1 tbsp. superfine sugar (the sweetness of life)
- » 1 tsp. orange peel zest

Embrace your power as you inhale the fragrance of the orange. Direct your will through the zester and into the orange to empower it.

Slice the orange in half and juice half. Picture any obstacles you encounter on your road to success being cut off. Slice the other half into wedges.

Place the wedges in the bottom of a heavy-bottomed glass or cocktail shaker. Sprinkle the superfine sugar over the oranges. Muddle while invoking the power of orange for creativity, fortune, and change.

Add orange vodka and ice. Shake the cocktail shaker vigorously while envisioning your new venture coming to fruition, for example, opening day of your new store, first day at the new job, or something similar.

Strain into a large brandy snifter. Add a pinch of zest and ice.

Enjoy while picturing yourself at your most successful.

 Sober Substitution: Juice your oranges and visualize your success. Buy orange juice, ground and center, then send the energy of success into the orange juice and drink.

Tool Substitutions: If you don't have a jigger handy to measure your alcohol, your standard shot glass holds 1.25 ounces of liquor, so measure carefully!

If you don't have a cocktail shaker, don't try two glasses; they could get stuck and cause an injury. Instead pour the ingredients into a thermos, cap, and shake!

If you don't have a juicer or a reamer for your citruses, don't try using a fork—that's a trip to the hospital waiting to happen. Squeeze the fruit by hand, or squeeze the fruit around a teaspoon if you want a little pulpy texture in your beverage.

If you don't have a bar spoon, use the handle end of a serving spoon; it'll be longer than the forks in the drawer and will stir the drink more at the bottom than the top, due to the common teardrop shape where the thumb rests.

If you don't have a Hawthorne strainer, use a tea ball to pour through. It'll pick up the large pieces and will hold back ice without robbing the drink of texture and foam.

PENTACLE-CUTTING BOARD

The extension of the pentacle is the altar because the pentacle is the microcosm of the macrocosm. The altar is a representation of the larger cosmos. The pentacle is a disk inscribed with the five-pointed star inside of a circle. This disk or plate is used for consecrating ritual items, including all of the tools for the altar before they are used in ritual the first time. Each point has a reference to something in the outer world: earth, air, fire, water, and spirit. In our bar tools, the pentacle is the cutting board, the place where our spirits take root in the physical world.

BAR CABINET AS ALTAR SPACE

Throughout your journey through this book, I'd love for you to have a space that is as magical as you are. I have an IKEA bar cabinet; you can use a cocktail cart, a secret boozy globe in your office, or just a kitchen cabinet shelf. When I say altar, many people picture a table covered with two hundred candles and an occasional rock. The altar space I'm talking about here is a sacred space to create the potions and brews that empower you. So however that looks, permit yourself to dedicate a space to exploring your expression of your tastes, feelings, and thoughts on each of these tools.

Wand—Fire—Muddler

Chalice—Water—Cup—Cocktail shaker

Pentacle—Earth—Cutting board

Sword—Air—Paring knife

Spirit—Alcoholic spirit of choice

Getting to Know
Your Allies

L earning the history and lore of these magical, plant-based beverages will help grow your understanding of the magical applications each has to offer. Rarely derived from a single plant source, the drinks originating from some of these plants can vary widely. But does that make them inherently magical? Yes and no.

ON SPIRITS, SPIRITS, AND INGREDIENTS

We associate beer, fermented things, and alcoholic drinks with the divine (and usually the divine feminine) because of the transformation they undergo. They go into the liminal space of the brewing vat and come out forever changed. As if by magic. Liminality, standing on the precipice of the doorway, of change.

Demonstrating this liminality is the heathen ritual of *symbel*, famously demonstrated in *Beowulf*, where the mead, cider, or beer is placed in a large horn to be shared among bonded people. The horn is a transformative object. The *byrelle* who carries the horn is responsible for maintaining the ritual harmony of the group and the flow of words over the horn. The taboo of lying over a horn is not just about the integrity of the group. That is a factor, but as words spoken over the horn are laid in the *Well of Wyrd,* they have a habit of becoming the truth. The Well of Wyrd is a concept that the things we do form the foundation of who we are. Each of those layers informs our personality, our life's circumstances, as well as our successes and failures. The horn is the liminal space because it goes into the horn as mead or cider, and comes out changed through the bond shared by all people. The same happens when the cup and chalice are used to enact the Great Rite (in token). Pouring magic into the chalice changes the contents. When a Catholic priest blesses wine in a large chalice for Communion, though we don't subscribe to transubstantiation per se, it's a similar idea.

In popular culture, the image of the byrelle has been reduced to the image of a barmaid, or the blonde figure of a famous beer brand. Women's past work with beer and brewing as a magical occupation has thousands of years of history behind it. The first brewers were women and continued the tradition of ale-wifery until the 1300s when men started moving from selling their wives' brews to passing laws to forbid them from brewing it.

Brewing kettles have been famously found in a woman's grave goods from a 1920s dig from 1370 BCE. She was barely 18 when she died and was buried with her most prized possessions, including a bucket made from tree bark in which to brew beer. Let the spark of magic in these spirits guide you on your magical journey.

ABSINTHE

Main Botanical: *Artemisia absinthium*

Botanical Family: Asteraceae

World Origin: North America, England, Kashmir Valley

Part of Plant Used: Leaves

Scent Description: Green, herbal

Scent Impact: Release of conscious thought, meditative, aphrodisiac, stimulant (discussion and free-thinking)

Related spirits: Vermouth

MAGICAL CORRESPONDENCES

Element: Water

Day: Monday

Magical Uses: Protection, divination, lust, love, invoking nature spirits, healing, sleep

Planet: Moon

Astrological Sign: Cancer

Suggested Crystal: Hematite

Deity/Spirit: Hecate, Diana

Warnings: Wormwood is an emmenagogue and abortifacient. Do not ingest if pregnant or nursing. It can increase flow in menstruating persons. The essential oil can cause seizures in those with a history of seizure.

HERBAL LORE AND USES

Even Shakespeare knew of the link between magic and wormwood. He illustrated the relationship between the Artemisia family and magic in *A Midsummer Night's Dream* when Oberon uses the herb to reverse the effects of the love potion.

Wormwood has a long and storied history. Wormwood beverages were thought to make men mad and were primarily associated with creative people and the pursuit of their arts. Absinthe itself is even a nom de guerre or pseudonym of wormwood itself—a singular name, although this drink contains several other botanicals, including anise seed, calamus, coriander, fennel, hyssop, licorice, melissa, and star anise. Let's look at the magical associations of the herbals contained in this potent brew.

- » Anise seed (protecting babies, increasing appetite, purification)
- » Calamus (commanding, balance, love, peace, compelling)
- » Coriander (clairvoyance, divination, property retention, healing)
- » Fennel (protection, healing, purification, warding off evil spirits)
- » Hyssop (sleep disorders, conception, growth)
- » Licorice (nourishing, road opening, endurance, fidelity, love, lust, being heard)
- » Melissa (love, fertility, antidepressant, compassion)
- » Star anise (contacting other planes, meditation, divination)

Thujone is the naturally occurring, active chemical constituent in wormwood that acts on the pleasure centers in the brain. Thujone is also found in *Salvia officianalis* (garden sage), as well as in the cedar family (Thuja), and tansy (*Tanacetum vulgare*). This chemical acts on the same region of the brain as marijuana and chocolate. But don't expect pink elephants to appear unless you're drinking this before bed.

Smoking wormwood or its plant cousin, mugwort (*Artemisia vulgaris*), is prevalent in areas of the world where absinthe is banned. Reported psychoactive effects include a relaxed feeling for the body and mind. However, I would not recommend smoking either plant; more research into drug interactions and contraindications should be done. Smoking wormwood and mugwort is unpleasant because they contain absinthin, among the most bitter of all compounds. In the United States and Europe, wormwood is mixed with mugwort for a meditative salve applied to pulse points. This is much gentler on the system, as long as you aren't pregnant, having liver problems, or experiencing other limiting factors.

The reputed link between absinthe and madness has to do with the potion being brewed in lead bathtubs during the drink's heyday. Modern brewing is much more hygienic. Legalized in the United States in July of 2007, after ninety-five years of prohibition, this mysterious beverage can now be enjoyed to its fullest.

Be aware, this drink averages between 120 and 160 proof. A bottle I obtained in the Czech Republic was made from distilled wine rather than spirits for a better taste and a natural drink. That bottle was 185 proof and came with a significant warning. The exotically herbal flavor is due in part to the nature of thujone, as a naturally occurring chemical related to camphor. When looking at the chemical's structure, it looks remarkably like camphor and menthol, and has the minty feeling that camphor and menthol have. Still, if you look at the way each element bonds to one another, it acts similarly to the tetrahydrocannabinol (THC) found in marijuana. It shouldn't surprise, after seeing the active ingredients work on the same regions of the brain, and in a similar manner.

Because of the high proof and bitter herbal taste, this licorice-like beverage is rarely consumed neat, and adherents of The Green Fairy develop elaborate rituals for consumption. The most common is to use ornate water fountains to drip iced water over sugar cubes and into the glass of absinthe to a ratio of 1:4 or 1:5 parts absinthe to water. It turns the clear green liquor to an emerald-colored milky delight due to the interaction of the water on the oils present in the distillate, namely fennel.

A more visually compelling method is popular in the Czech Republic: the sugar cube is dipped in the high-proof alcohol, placed on the absinthe spoon, and lit to caramelize the sugar. The flaming cube is then (carefully) added to the glass, and ice water is then poured into the drink to put out the fire in the glass. As always, use common sense when considering incorporating alcohol and fire. If you don't own an absinthe spoon and are not sure about procuring one, using superfine sugar that will dissolve easily in the solution is preferred. Traditional table sugar is difficult to dissolve in cold water.

PRACTICAL USES

Yes, you can empower and drink absinthe for the below-listed intentions; this will give you some alternatives. For most of the noningestion uses, you can find cheap absinthe because if you aren't drinking it, it won't matter how it tastes. Just make sure it has a proof over 99 if the working involves fire.

Antianxiety and antidepressant—Spread a teaspoon or tablespoon of superfine sugar on a plate or cutting board. Spell out the source of your anxiety or depressive episode if known in the sugar. If unknown, write "anxiety" or "depression" in the sugar using your finger as your wand. Empower the sugar with your touch. Pour the sugar into the absinthe, stir to dissolve, and add ice water until reaching the desired 1:4 or 1:5 ratio of absinthe to water. See the source of anxiety dissolving. If symptoms persist, consider talk therapy, there are many free resources, in person, via phone, and even text-based.

 Sober Substitution: Pour the sugar into an herbal tea containing licorice.

Binding, defense, or banishing—Write the name of the offender and crime on a piece of rice paper. Dip the piece of paper in absinthe and eat. As the edible paper is digested and passed, so too will they pass from your life and influence. Absinthe is powerful defensive magic; the bitterness reminds us to take the magic seriously.

A cautionary note: *Binding and banishing are two different ritual actions, although they carry similar associations. Binding can keep the* *target from harming, but can tie them to you. In many settings and situations, it can be critical to banish them or cast a spell for them to be caught and punished so that the next person is safe as well.*

Love, lust—Wormwood, calamus, licorice, anise, and hyssop all have associations of the Venusian variety. Allow this to be a partner exercise. Grab two (more for additional partners) sugar cubes, absinthe, and glasses. Each person holds a sugar cube in their nondominant hand. Press the dominant palms together and link fingers so that the pad of the thumb is between the hands. The large thumb mound of the palm is the Mount of Venus in palmistry. This gets more intricate with more than two partners but bear with me. Have your partner kiss your sugar cube and think of love, lust, and the like. Place the sugar on the absinthe spoon and start dripping ice water onto your cube, while thinking romantic things. This working can also be useful solo for asexual or aromantic persons to practice self-love and self-worth.

Accident avoidance—Made of many strong allies, absinthe is a potent power. Bless your home, automobile, and other items to avoid accidents in the house, or while inside the car, truck, or on the motorcycle. Pour a shot of absinthe after cleansing your home with smoke, floor washes, or sweeping powders. Starting at the point farthest from the main entrance, and working clockwise outward, anoint the windows and exterior doors. A little dab will do you, but feel free to use protective symbols if feeling called to do so. If anointing a vehicle, start outside at the front fender and move clockwise around it, hitting all sides. Don't anoint the inside as a) most accidents are coming from outside the car, and b) we don't want the interior of the vehicle to smell like alcohol. The alcohol will evaporate, leaving behind a trace amount of the oils that are present in the liquor, so stick to metal surfaces or test in an inconspicuous spot to make sure there is no damage to paint. Don't forget the tires too! Road hazards like rocks, screws, and more cause more than their fair share of accidents.

Increasing psychic ability—Closely linked to psychic ability, dream work, and crossing the hedge, absinthe and wormwood put you in touch with other senses and other realms. Whether you're interested in astral travel, deep meditative states, or improving your lottery predictions, the Artemisia family has your back. A single serving of absinthe can inspire a peaceful, dream-filled sleep, lull you into a meditative state, or put you into an altered state of consciousness. If you'd prefer to work sober but have no issues with alcohol, you can put 1:10 ratio absinthe to water into a water bottle and spritz the air in your work space. You'll have the aromatic effect of the wormwood and the other aromatics, without the impact of alcohol or the smoke of burning wormwood or mugwort. If you fear for white rugs or light-colored furniture, use a 1:20 ratio and add a drop of fennel and a drop of hyssop essential oil.

Avoid fennel if pregnant or nursing. Avoid hyssop if you have a history of seizures. You can replace one or both of these essential oils with rosemary.

Seeing Spirits Summoning—For connecting to the afterlife and the dead, anoint a black or white candle with absinthe and allow it to dry. Don't light while it is still wet; the alcohol content is *highly flammable*. Carve the name of the deceased loved one into the candle with a candle scribe, a ballpoint pen, or a nail. Include birthdate if known. Consider adding a photograph if you have one. If framed, position the photo in the frame so that you can see the flame of the candle reflected in the photo's glass. Make sure it is far enough away to safely stand and not present a fire hazard. If the ancestor is unknown, write "ancestor" or some similar significator. Burn on a Friday if the ancestor is beloved; otherwise, burn on a Saturday, the day associated with the dead. While the candle burns, meditate on their face, their name, or their connection to you while you await your message.

"You've Got This" Resolving Anger Spell—Dig out a cauldron or sturdy pot for this one. Wormwood is useful for resolving anger, transformation, and endurance. It will lift the burden and weight of the rage while shoring up your defenses against any future onslaught. Grab some paper and a pen; make it a red one if you have it. Let your anger burn hotly, and write all your frustration out. Start with the issue at hand and branch out to anything causing frustration, anger, or irritation as those smaller issues can add up. Write it out, draw a picture if it is helpful, pour it out on the pages. Once you're finished, lightly crumple the paper into a ball. Make sure there is enough space in the ball for air to get in there; otherwise, the paper won't burn well. Whether you have one piece of paper or ten, stack them in the cauldron. Walk outside, or go on the patio, fire escape, or the balcony. Don't set off the fire alarm inside. Grab a shot of absinthe and douse the paper. (Make sure the proof is 100 or more. Less than that, and your paper won't burn.) Light! See all of those frustrations, irritations, and issues go up in smoke. Make sure you have your cauldron or pot lid handy in case the contained fire gets out of hand. Safety first, otherwise you have a different set of problems.

> **Sober Substitution:** Make your list, crumple the papers into loose ball shapes, and sprinkle with dried wormwood or mugwort. Ignite.

Protection against the Fae, Faeries, the Good Neighbors—The Fae are a popular topic among new age circles, but there are a good deal more stories of Faerie where humans either don't live to the end or make out poorly. There is a reason people leave out butter and cream; they're paying protection money to the Faerie mafia, so they don't try to come in the house. Gotta pay off the Mab.

To protect your home and property from the Fae, mix 1 part absinthe, 5 parts water, and rust in a bottle. (You can throw a rusty nail in there if that's all you have. Iron oxide is also sold online from scientific supply companies.) Walk the boundaries of your property with your mixture, splashing the property lines with the combination. Feel free to sing a boundary song if you like. This spell works best on the Summer Solstice or a Sunday. Added oomph: after the first pass around the boundary, bless four railroad spikes with absinthe mixture and pound all four spikes into the ground (below ground level, so they don't stick up and hurt someone mowing the grass, if you have any). Feel free to incorporate other *beating the bounds* magic, like carrying a lit torch or banging a drum at the borders of your property. If you suspect an infestation, reclaim your property before the bounds beating by urinating in a bucket and letting it sit undisturbed for twenty-four hours (where it can't get knocked over accidentally) then dump it on your front porch, claiming the space as yours. If you're terribly squicked out by the thought of it, grab a bottle of ammonia from the store, spit in it, put the cap on it, shake, and dump it on the porch.

Banishing disharmony and purification—Grab a bucket, a scrubbing broom or sponge, a hose, and strong soap, as well as absinthe. This is best done on a sunny day. Place a squirt of soap in the bucket—lemon (protection) dish soap is great for this if you don't have something in mind. Add a splash of absinthe or three drops of wormwood essential oil as a sober substitution (because it's a well-ventilated area). Scrub all the windows you can reach like you mean it. Through all the energy you expend cleaning the house, visualize removal of the disharmony, hexes, and the like.

Dreaming of a future lover—Wormwood has long been associated with inducing visions. To have peaceful dreams divining the face of your true love, a prospective partner, or the like, ritually prepare absinthe for drinking with sugar and water. Draw the energy of the earth into your hands, and press the energy into the milky green liquid. You are empowering the drink for your highest good. Drink directly before bed.

 Sober Substitution: Prepare an incense of ½ part marigold flowers, 2 parts thyme, 1 part marjoram, and 2 parts sandalwood. Burn in the bedroom one-half hour before bed so the fire can be safely extinguished before retiring for the night. It will also give the room time to air out, so the smell still permeates the room but won't cause sleep anxiety surrounding the quest for rest.

Peace, care for the dying—One of the hardest, and most rewarding, things we as humans can do for one another is to sit at the bedside of someone who is dying. I sat at the bedside of my "mom," a woman my family called Peep. I dedicated my previous book, *Blackthorn's Botanical Magic,* to her. She was already in hospice when I got the contract for my first book. I was able to tell her, but she was unresponsive by that point. She died the next day. Wormwood and mugwort are boundary plants. They can reinforce boundaries, or leave them a smoldering ruin. They can help you cross the hedge, or hide you from view. For a loved one who is dying, you can get permission in the manner that suits the situation, and anoint their hands and feet with a small amount of absinthe (in a roller bottle is just fine). The person may be lucid enough to welcome wormwood or mugwort salve. It is a soothing sedative that encourages restful sleep and the happiest dreams of their loved ones. It gently opens the door to the other side. As they near death, they may start to see loved ones who have crossed over. There is nothing to fear there. Peep started seeing her departed husband three days before she died. I also anointed myself after I got home from caretaking missions. You may have days where you decide to anoint your insides as well. (Always in moderation, of course.) No judgment here. My most cherished sister, author H. Byron Ballard, reminds people in her lectures that aromatherapy is being more understood and accepted in hospitals, so the aromatic effect of wormwood can be utilized here as well. Make a strong infusion of wormwood in water and soak cotton balls in it with a drop or two of lavender. Most nurses know about lavender oil being calming for patients. The loved one can smell the cotton balls, as it helps calm, open that door to loved ones, and aids their crossing the veil.

Attracting tutelary spirits—Wormwood's reputation for helping people to see visions also lends itself to the realms of nature and the unseen. Wormwood can attract the beneficial spirits with something to teach and improves our ability to see them. This ability extends to elementals as well: gnomes, sylphs, salamanders, and undines. To attract these beneficial spirits, leave out offerings of absinthe or dried wormwood, or burn wormwood or mugwort as incense during meditation. You might also consider connecting with the land wights or the spirits of place where you live.

Laying a hex—The topic of hexing can be very polarizing. People may assume I'm advocating putting the time and energy into cursing everyone that ever looked crossways at me or may have overblown fears of scary ingredients like the eye of a newt and toe of frog. Banishing a harmful person from your life requires intent and a few tools. Laying a hex with wormwood has the added benefit of bringing happiness and relieving anxiety for the caster. Pour half a shot of absinthe, and fill the rest of the shot glass with simple syrup (chilled if possible). Hold the shot to your lips, whisper their name across the surface of the liquid, and state your intended outcome. Drink. Make sure you feel the energy, to empower the working.

Sweetening someone's disposition—Absinthe can be a bonding experience and a friendly gesture. If there is someone in your life who seems to sour at your presence, consider sharing absinthe with them to talk out any past issues. It is antianxiety, antidepressant, lifts mood, and counters misfortune. It could be that you are projecting anxiety onto the situation. Remember, fear is not intuition. If there is an issue you are unaware of, this is an excellent chance to bond and work out any missteps. If you're too shy to approach them for a night out, you have options. You can buy a bottle and invite other coworkers to your place, where there is safety and comfort, and make it a group wellness exercise.

You can also make a paper poppet of the person in question, place it in a jar, and "feed" it honey to get the person to act with less hatred towards you. Cut out a gingerbread man shape and name it with the person's full name and (if you have it) any biographical data like date, time, and place of birth. If some of your data is missing, try to be descriptive, "Bob from accounting," "the jerk in 3B." Jars are a long-term working, but work rapidly. Place Paper Bob in the jar and pour honey over the doll. (Really any sweetener will work: simple syrup, waffle syrup, molasses . . .) Talk to it and say the things you wish you were empowered to say to Bob directly. Occasionally add more sugar or honey and keep talking to the jar. Feel free to put the lid on and burn candles over the jar between chats between you and the jar to empower it.

RECIPES

Absinthe can be a harsh mistress so try to stick to a more delightful bottle of absinthe for drinking and save the cheap stuff for sprinkling, workings, and the occasional offering. I really enjoy Vieux Carre out of Philadelphia. It has a lovely sweet tea finish, and it was the first distillery in the United States to be granted a license after the ban on creating authentic absinthe was lifted. Before 2007, there were bottles of a bitter, licorice-flavored liquor for sale, but it did not contain the *Artemisia absinthium* needed for it to qualify as true absinthe.

Absinthe came to popularity in France after a disastrous blight attacked the old-world grape varieties and decimated the wine country. The Great French Grape Blight was beneficial for winemakers in Argentina and other parts of the world. This fungus, similar to the late blight fungus that hit Ireland, leading to the Great Potato Famine, is thought to have arrived in 1858, but by the mid-1860s was a full-on disaster. With the scarcity of available wines, distilled spirits like absinthe came into vogue.

Sazerac

This is one of the quintessential absinthe cocktails. The wide variety of magical associations for this drink lend it to many magical intentions. It can be used for protection from night terrors, a love potion (happiness plus love can draw the right lover to you), the transformation of pain, binding desire (if you have feelings you don't want), increasing psychic visions, recovering after a magical attack, and many more.

Tools

- » 2 glasses, one a cocktail glass
- » Optional: atomizer
- » Strainer

Ingredients

- » 2 oz. rye whiskey (prosperity, fertility, love, beauty)
- » Ice
- » 1 tsp. ice water
- » An absinthe rinse (dreams, hex breaking, psychic power, happiness, healing, initiation)
- » 2 dashes Peychaud's Bitters (desire, fertility, power, protection, inner growth, combatting chronic pain and illness, recovering from illness or travel)
- » 1 sugar cube (love, lust, mood-elevating, sex magic)
- » 1 strip of lemon peel for garnish (calm, clarity, increase spell's power, divination, banish fatigue, fidelity, protection, abundance)

Rinse the cocktail glass with absinthe or spritz it from a cocktail atomizer. Atomizers are excellent to use if you enjoy a whisper of vermouth in your martini as it is less wasteful than rinsing. In the other glass place sugar, bitters, and water. Stir the glass with the sugar to ensure it is dissolved. Add ice and whiskey to the sugar glass. Let sit for a moment to chill the whiskey without watering it down, then strain into the cocktail glass. Express lemon over the surface of the liquid and garnish. Enjoy while visualizing your set intention. Remember to take conscious breaths between sips (in through the nose, out through the mouth), to help keep you centered.

AMARETTO

Main Botanical: Apricot (Prunus armeniaca)

Botanical Family: Rosaceae

World Origin: Turkey, Uzbekistan, Italy, Algeria, Iran

Part of Plant Used: Stone

Scent Description: Woody, sweet

Scent Impact: Calm, loving thoughts

MAGICAL CORRESPONDENCES

Element: Fire

Day: Sunday

Magical Uses: Lust, love, longevity, healing, peace

Planet: Sun

Astrological Sign: Cancer

Suggested Crystal: Hematite

Deity/Spirit: Aphrodite

Warnings: Do not ingest bitter apricot seeds. They contain *amygdalin*, which is processed in the body as cyanide. *Seizures, respiratory failure, and death can occur.*

HERBAL LORE AND USES

Disaronno Amaretto is known for the almond flavoring it adds to drinks, but that signature flavor comes from the sweet pit of Mediterranean apricot seeds, rather than almonds. Cultivation of apricots started in China (as did the predecessors of the modern citruses) around 4000 BCE. They didn't arrive in England for another four thousand years.

As apricots are a member of the rose family (as are all stone fruit), it should be no surprise that these tasty fruits are used in love magic. That's not all these magical powerhouses are known to possess.

PRACTICAL USES

Most of these can use dried apricots for **Sober Substitutions.**

Creativity—Sprinkle Amaretto over paintbrushes, pens, and other tools of the creative spark to reinvigorate the creative drive.

Sober Substitution: Snack on dried apricots when feeling low energy or a lack of creativity.

Turning aside evil—Anoint yourself with Amaretto on forehead, throat, heart, hands, and feet to banish evil from your presence. After house cleansings, anoint doors and windows with a drop of Amaretto to seal the home against corruption.

Sober Substitution: Place a pinch of ground apricot seed in the four corners of the house.

Knowledge of goodness—Anoint the forehead with Amaretto or apricot kernel oil to allow and preserve the knowledge of the good in people and the universe.

Sober Substitution: Substitute apricot kernel oil for Amaretto.

Love—Massage a partner with apricot kernel oil to remind them of the loving connection you share.

Passion—Pour your partner a shot of Amaretto and add it to orange juice to boost intensity and creativity in your relationship. Share the drink (works best when skyclad/nude).

Opening the mind—To expand consciousness, add a shot of Amaretto to a lemon-lime soda. Lemon is calming and useful for divination. Lime is appropriate for overcoming powerlessness and increasing focus. Enjoy while taking relaxing breaths.

Relaxation—Curl up with dried apricots and, as you nibble them, see your cares disappearing.

Distrust—Talk to your friends and partners. Communication is the remedy for distrust if it can be remedied. Share Amaretto or dried apricots with them while you speak about past behaviors and ways to build trust in the future.

Peace or healing—Anoint the forehead with apricot kernel oil. Fill a 10 ml roller bottle with a drop of lavender essential oil and fill with apricot kernel oil. Write "peace" or "healing" on arms and legs and massage into skin. Breathe in through the nose and out through the mouth while doing so.

Healing love relationship—Add ground apricot kernels to an incense of 2 parts cardamom and 1 part cinnamon. Burn in a well-ventilated area; cinnamon can irritate the lungs.

RECIPES

Amaretto Sour, Love Sweeting

Tools

» Cocktail shaker

» Strainer

» Cocktail glass

» An old-fashioned glass

Ingredients

» 2 oz. Disaronno Amaretto (love, passion, knowledge, open mind)

» 1 oz. lemon juice (calming, ability, friendship, purification, fidelity)

» 1 egg white (fertility)

» A dash of Angostura bitters (fertility, desire, power, inner growth, love)

» A cherry for garnish

Into a cocktail shaker add ice, 2 shots of Amaretto, a shot of lemon, and an egg white (a widemouthed plastic bottle can be used to pick up an unbroken egg yolk with a little practice). Cap the shaker and shake vigorously until frost forms on the metal. It'll give the white time to *cook* in the lemon juice and break up against the ice cubes.

Strain into another cocktail glass and discard the ice. Return liquid to the shaker and repeat the shaking process without ice. Envision loving relationship blossoming. The second shake will add the foam needed for the drink's signature look and texture as well as magical energy.

Put ice into an old-fashioned glass and pour the cocktail over it.

Drink while envisioning the desired effect.

BEER

Main Botanical: Barley (Hordeum vulgare)

Botanical Family: Poaceae

World Origin: Middle East

Part of Plant Used: Seeds

Scent Description: Earthy, warm

Scent Impact: N/A

MAGICAL CORRESPONDENCES

Element: Earth

Day: Friday

Magical Uses: Aphrodisiac, fertility, potency, prosperity, lust

Planet: Venus

Astrological Signs: Libra (contemporary), Taurus (ancient)

Suggested Crystal: Jaspers

Deity/Spirit: Demeter, Diana

Warnings: Do not consume large amounts of barley during pregnancy, whether or not it is fermented.

HERBAL LORE AND USES

Historians have been able to trace the lineage of fermentation to before 9000 BCE. The debate is mostly whether barley's use in bread or fermentation led to the establishment of civilization at that time. By growing barley and other cereal grains in the grass family, early people were capable of domesticating cattle and other animals, as well as developing codes of conduct. By 2900 BCE, civilizations like ancient Sumer were brewing beers and dedicating poems to goddesses like Ninsaki, the goddess of brewing. In 2400 BCE, the straw was invented to drink beer more efficiently. Established guides for brewing beer as well as how to serve it are among the oldest written laws, the Code of Hammurabi, dated to1760 BCE.

Since beer is made with malted (or sprouted) barley, it is possible, nay, likely that the first beers were an accident of invention. Barley left in wet conditions sprouts readily. Planting sprouts rather than seeds means less wasted labor, as there are no dead seeds planted. Anything that didn't germinate could be placed in the mash bucket. Fermentation is a by-product of natural yeasts, both in the air and on living things, and nature took it from there.

PRACTICAL USES

Love drawing—Barley's Venusian associations make it the perfect candidate for workings to attract the right lover. On a Friday, find a barley wine (high in sugar content and alcohol content; enjoy responsibly) and sit out under the moon, if possible. Ask for the blessings of Demeter, who is so beloved by Zeus she receives the first and the best of the offerings. You deserve the best. You deserve a healthy relationship. After listing qualities needed in the perfect person, open the beer. Anoint the forehead for thinking of the ideal person. Anoint the heart for the heart connection to that person. Anoint the hands to receive their love. Anoint your feet to lead you to them. Pour the rest of the beer on the ground, in the garden, or at the base of a tree (it makes excellent fertilizer) in thanks to Demeter.

Money—The earthly plane is full of material goods, and sadly, barter isn't as common as it should be. To increase your prosperity, gather a bowl, matches, a candleholder with matching candle, and a bottle of beer. Votive candles and candleholders are ideal for this. On a Thursday for prosperity, place the candleholder into the bowl and pour in the beer surrounding the candleholder. If candle color is crucial to you, grab something green for fertility or brown for stability. Using a pen or candle scribe, draw a $ on the candle, and write your name if you have space. Bless the candle with olive oil for prosperity. Light. Allow the candle to burn all the way down, if possible. Fire safety is more important than continuity, so blow it out if you have to leave. "But, won't I be blowing the money/blessings away?" No, the candle is still there. If you prefer a candle snuff, that's your call. Don't let fear rule your magical choices. When the candle is burned down, feel free to toss the candle remains and leave the barley or pour the beer outside in nature.

> **Sober Substitution**: Use barley from the grocery store in the bowl instead of beer. Feel free to add a bit of water to the barley to keep it fire safe, and remember to dispose of it in nature before it ferments.

Fertility—When trying to conceive a baby, barley aids both healing and sexual potency and drive. Barley is also used to bless weddings. The partners trying to conceive can choose to bathe together or separately (a rosemary infusion makes an excellent, holy bath for this work). At the end of the bath, each should pour a cup of beer over their head. It also removes product buildup from the hair and leaves it weightless and shiny.

Banishing poverty—On a Saturday (endings), gather a handful of barley in your dominant hand. Name the grain with the source of your debt, "joblessness," "medical bills," and the like. Envision your debt crumbling into dust and being blown away. Cast the barley into a fire and watch it disappear.

Offerings—Both beer and barley have been used as offerings for gods since before recorded history to ask for a favor or to give thanks for previous blessings. It can also be used to honor the spirits or gods that have seen you through a difficult time; barley is a beautiful way to say, "Thank you." Speak from the heart. Then, take the grain out into nature, or leave a custard cup of it on your altar for three days before casting it outside.

Funerals—Associated with death and the dead, beer and barley have long been offered in ceremonies celebrating life. Toasting a life well lived is the spirit of this drink. It is a common practice to open a beer for a loved one that has crossed the veil. It can sit open for upwards of three days before the spirit has gone out of the drink and can be poured outside for the plant life.

RECIPES

Repairing Radler

This half beer, half soda concoction was developed in Bavaria. The drink was aimed at bicyclists during the Roaring Twenties when the cycling craze was first taking off. An ingenious bar owner had thirteen thousand cyclists show up for a drink during a hot June day in 1922. He quickly realized he was going to run out of beer, so he started making the concoction to use up the soda he had lying around. It was supposed to quench the thirst worked up in the heat. Today it's closely associated with the shandy. The magical associations of both the drinks are love and friendship, so it makes it the perfect drink for bonding with friends and smoothing over any bumps in the road, arguments, fights, or misunderstandings. This will also help protect the bond in the future.

Tools

>   » Pint glass

Ingredients

>   » 12 oz. beer—something with a light taste (love, healing)

>   » 4 oz. lemon-lime soda (friendship, purification, protection)

Slowly pour the beer into the glass to avoid a head of foam. Fill the glass with lemon-lime soda.

Peppermint Perception

Peppermint is linked to intuition, perception, psychic abilities, and more. If you have a friend who seems to be going through something difficult, reach out and make time for them. Prepare this tasty drink and invite them to unburden themselves.

Tools

» Pint glass

Ingredients

» 12 oz. pale lager, chilled

» 1 oz. peppermint schnapps

Pour the schnapps into the glass first, and slowly add the beer afterward so that the drink will mix gently.

Sober Substitution: Invite them over, make a big pot of peppermint tea (perhaps with a barley soup), and let them settle in for comfort and reassurance.

HOPS (HUMULUS LUPULUS)

Botanical Family: Cannabaceae

World Origin: Southwest Asia, England, North America

Part of Plant Used: Flower

Scent Description: Citrusy, green

Scent Impact: Soothing, restorative

MAGICAL CORRESPONDENCES

Element: Water

Day: Monday

Magical Uses: Nourishment, sleep, dreams, grounding, healing, justice, protection

Planet: Moon

Astrological Sign: Cancer

Suggested Crystal: Moonstone

Deity/Spirit: Selene

Warnings: Sedative. Do not combine with other sedatives. It can cause dangerous reactions.

HERBAL LORE AND USES

Young shoots and leaves of the hops plant were prepared and eaten like asparagus by the Romans. This bitter flower is a powerful sedative, and infusions of hops in water are used to stave off sleeplessness. Pillows stuffed with hops have been prescribed to insomniacs for thousands of years. It also is a powerful stress reliever.

The addition of hops to beer is what allowed this beverage to be transported over long distances. Because of its antibacterial properties, it preserved the beer for longer shelf life.

PRACTICAL USES

Sleep—Prepare a small pouch, prepurchased or hand-sewn, whichever suits your needs (as a last resort, paper and a stapler will work). Fill the bag with dried hops and ask for the blessings of sleep. Pass the bag through the four elements by breathing on it, anointing it with saltwater, and passing it over a candle flame (not through—safety first). Place the pillow inside your pillowcase and sleep well. Bonus: Add a pinch of dried mugwort or dried wormwood for extra oomph.

Balance—To restore balance in a home, carefully light incense charcoal, place a pinch of hops on the coals, and cleanse the house with the smoke. Consider adding a frankincense tear for blessings of spirit, or dragon's blood for protection.

Prophetic dreams—Prepare an infusion of hops, 1 teaspoon of dried flower to 8 ounces boiling water. Let steep for 5 minutes and sweeten if desired, as hops are quite bitter. Drink 30 minutes before bed. As you drift off to sleep, concentrate on the area in which you need guidance.

Focus—Prepare an infusion of hops, 1 teaspoon of dried flower to 8 ounces boiling water. Let steep for 5 minutes. Strain hop flowers from the infusion. Pour infusion into an aromatherapy diffuser. Add a single drop of basil (avoid if you have a history of seizures), ginger, or black pepper essential oil to increase focus. If this is a long-term project, alternate oils in the diffuser as we can become nose-blind to the oil quickly.

Grounding—If feeling scattered, light charcoal and burn a pinch of hops flowers with clove buds, or ground clove from the spice rack. Sit in front of the censer while taking slow, meditative breaths, in through the nose, and out through the mouth.

Healing—Both the healing and protective powers of hops make it an ideal ally for a broken heart. To that end, prepare an infusion of hops, 1 teaspoon of dried flower to 8 ounces boiling water. Let steep for 5 minutes. Strain out the flowers, and, in sacred space, anoint your temples to heal your mind. Anoint your lips to speak well of yourself. Anoint your throat to protect your voice and make it heard. Anoint your heart to heal and learn to stand up for yourself. Anoint your belly to remind yourself that love and survival should be separated. (Romantic love is not necessary for survival; survival comes first. We can't make another you.) Anoint your feet to protect your ability to walk away from harmful situations.

Seeing justice served—If court papers are involved, make a copy of them; if you have a photo, even better. Grab a jar with a lid, a cup of hoppy beer, jasmine flowers (justice), patchouli leaves (Just Judge), sandalwood (purifying, justice) or sandalwood incense, and black peppercorns (energy, focus, clear speech). Any combination of the above will work. Feel free to omit anything you don't have or can't get. Grab a plate or a bowl as well as a candle. Suggestions include a black candle for banishing, white for the purity of intention, or brown for a long-lasting magical effect. Place the jar in the bowl, then place a handful of peppercorns around it to protect you from the subject. In the jar place their photo (social media is excellent for this). If you have a copy of court documents, fold them and place in the jar. If you want a judge to see things your way, shred them with your bare hands (if possible) if you think the just thing is to banish the case before it goes to court. Place herbal materials in the jar, and pour in the beer. Close the jar. Place a candle on top of the jar if safe to do so; if not, next to the jar is just fine. Light the candle you've chosen on a Sunday for fiery protection, Monday for peace of mind, Wednesday to communicate your feelings on the case, or Saturday to banish the case before it goes to court. In all cases, know that justice will be done. There is no room for doubt.

Sober Substitution: Replace beer with hops infusion. Prepare an infusion of hops using 1 teaspoon of dried flower to 8 ounces boiling water. Let steep for 5 minutes then strain out the herbs.

Prayers for physical healing—Burn hops over incense charcoal while the smoke lifts your prayers for the health and healing of you, your friend, or loved one. Consider adding other herbs to improve the smell of the incense as well as magical function. Add clove for luck and happiness, cedar for physical strength, or rosemary for joy and harmony.

Relaxation—Hops are a powerful sedative; they can provide a restful respite during trying times. This is one of the reasons beer is associated with relaxing after a stressful day or strenuous labor; it is physically as well as emotionally sedating. Prepare an infusion of hops, 1 teaspoon of dried flower to 8 ounces boiling water. Let steep for 5 minutes then strain out the plant material. Sweeten if desired; hops are bitter. Slowly sip the infusion while breathing deeply of the aroma. Feel yourself relaxing, lowering your shoulders, and releasing tension in the body.

RECIPES

Outer Limits Intuition

This beverage has the lower alcohol content of a Shandy or a Radler, but rather than lemonade or lemon-lime soda, this is blended with ginger beer (no, not really a beer) for a hint of spice to go with that citrusy bite of hops.

Tools

» Beer mug

Ingredients

» 6 oz. India Pale Ale of your choice (prophetic dreams, elemental magic, relaxation)

» 6 oz. ginger beer (astral projection, power, magical strength, protection)

Pour the chilled IPA into a beer mug, just out of the freezer. Add the 6 oz. of ginger beer. (I used the super spicy Blenheim ginger ale for this, so the drink didn't feel watered down with ginger.) Enjoy while sitting in a comfortable spot, preferably in the shade of a tree on a beautiful day. Let your mind drift to the outer rings of Saturn, or somewhere else. See what information comes back to you.

BOURBON

(Also corn liquor, a.k.a. moonshine)

Main Botanical: Corn (Zea mays)

Botanical Family: Poaceae (grasses)

World Origin: Mexico, North America (Illinois, Indiana, Kentucky)

Part of Plant Used: Seeds

Scent Description: Sweet, dry

Scent Impact: N/A

MAGICAL CORRESPONDENCES

Element: Fire

Day: Sunday

Magical Uses: Protection, invoking nature spirits, blessing

Planet: Sun

Astrological Sign: Leo

Suggested Crystal: Carnelian

Deity/Spirit: Demeter (all cereal grains), Corn Mother (Selu in Tsalagi)

Warnings: None.

HERBAL LORE AND USES

Corn has been a part of Central and North American indigenous religions for eons. The pre-Columbian Americas worshipped the Corn Mother in the most widely spread geographic area, revered by Aztecs, Mayans, and Incans. The Quiché Mayas, the Navajo, and the Cherokee have stories of the first people being born of corn. These stories are more beautiful than I can do justice to, and I implore you to seek out indigenous storytellers for these moving tales.

After the settlers arrived in the new world, they started growing whatever staples they could use to feed themselves. Corn grew easily on the hand-cleared land, and it didn't mind the occasional tree stump in the way. Invented after settlers' harvests, corn beer made its debut. It was a quick way to use corn that would otherwise be wasted due to rot. It is only a hop, skip, and a jump from corn beer to corn whiskey.

Bourbon is an American whiskey made from corn rather than wheat, rye, or barley. This spirit is still barrel-aged like its Scottish and Irish counterparts. It became synonymous with Kentucky after the Virginia Land Law took effect, giving sixty-acre parcels to anyone who could grow corn on a plot of land, no matter who was living there at the time (read: indigenous people). Kentucky residents realized they could use laws like this to secure homesteads and figured out the way to handle large amounts of corn.

BOURBON VS. WHISKEY VS. WHISKY

The term whiskey is a title of a group of spirits rather than a single type of spirit. They are all barrel-aged, usually in an oak barrel that has been scorched on the inside to open the pores and allow color and flavor to permeate the brew. The distillation methods, as well as ingredients, will decide the type of whiskey it is. The two spellings come from translating Scots Gaelic and Irish languages (remember the countries with E in the name will add it to whiskey, IrEland, UnitEd StatEs).

The age of the whiskey, 8, 12, 18, 21 years, refers to the length of time it has been aging in a barrel, not how long it has been sitting in a glass bottle. Once it is bottled, the aging process stops.

Bourbon—Usually made in Kentucky, it can be made anywhere in the United States. It is made from corn.

Whiskey—Irish in nature, this spirit can also be made in the United States but stays true to the spirit of the Irish recipes. Included in this family is Tennessee Whiskey, which has its own history and flavor profile, similar to Irish, but not related to Kentucky bourbon.

Whisky—Without the "e" is the Scottish spelling for barrel-aged liquor that uses a base of fermented grains. Japan and Canada use it, too. Though these three countries share the spelling, each one has stringent rules about what constitutes a whisky.

PRACTICAL USES

Many of these uses can be made sober friendly by using corn kernels, corn flour, or cornmeal.

Fertility—Place a custard cup of bourbon under the bed for fertility during lovemaking.

Sober Substitution: Use dried corn kernels or a tablespoon of corn flour.

Prosperity/abundance—Anoint the inside of a glass or pottery jar with a lid with bourbon. At the end of the day, place loose change and small bills in the jar while asking for prosperity. Once or twice a year, empty the pot and place half in the bank account to bless the wealth you have. Take the other half and do something fun. You deserve it.

Sober Substitution: Coat your dominant palm in corn flour then coat the inside of the jar. Using your dominant pointer finger, inscribe symbols you associate with prosperity, such as dollar signs ($) and the like.

Agreement—Signing a contract and celebrating the agreement with bourbon is a custom in parts of the world where this liquor is found; however, if the other person isn't ready to agree, spell out the source of contention in the contract in corn flour. Sprinkle corn flour on a surface like a wooden cutting board (grounding) and in the flour—drawing a dollar sign, a heart for love, or a single word with your finger is enough. Charge the flour to find the middle ground. Then take the cutting board outside to scatter the intention to the four winds and bring air to the argument. You will come to an agreement within three days. Avoid drawing the symbol *with* the flour, as this is a practice for African Diaspora religions and their practices are their own. Alternatively, anoint a copy of the contract with bourbon to make it magically binding.

Mental acuity—Whether studying for a test or blocked for ideas for an important presentation, having a sharp mind is the key to success. To improve your focus, anoint pulse points with bourbon. Rosemary helps too! Place one drop rosemary in a 10 ml roller bottle, and fill with (cheap) bourbon. Cap roller bottle and apply to pulse points as needed.

> **Sober Substitution**: Substitute rubbing alcohol for the bourbon. Place a dried corn kernel and a drop of rosemary essential oil in the roller bottle, and fill with rubbing alcohol.

Blessing crops—These days, it's more and more likely to find someone with a back or front yard vegetable garden or a tomato plant in a pot on a patio. No matter your type of agriculture, bless the start of the season and your (eventual) harvest with a libation of bourbon, corn liquor, or cornmeal. You can pour a small amount into the soil before the first planting and sprinkle corn liquor on containers for gardening.

> **Sober Substitution**: Place a handful of cornmeal in the bottom of the planter or on the soil before tilling.

Evocation—To call forth nature spirits, or honor the gifts of Mother Nature, bless the bourbon or corn kernels by directing energy to them and knowing they are sacred. To recognize the spirits of nature, pour out offerings while singing, praying, or reciting poetry extolling their virtues. (Who doesn't want to hear beautiful things said about themselves?)

Balance—To restore balance within a home, take a custard cup of bourbon and set it in a sunny window for 3, 9, 33, or 99 minutes to absorb the solar energy. Using your hands, a pastry brush, or a tree branch as an asperger, dip into the bourbon and sprinkle it around the interior and exterior of a home. Be careful around light-colored fabrics.

> *Asperging (to asperge): the ritual action of utilizing a tool to sprinkle water or other liquids to cleanse and purify a space.*

Disagreement—There comes a time in friendships where there can be disagreements, arguments, or even a (verbal) fight. (If this is a pattern, you might want to examine the relationship for signs of abuse.) To clear the air and bring balance to the relationship after a disagreement, pour a shot of bourbon. Both parties hold the single shot together with their dominant hand. The Mount of Venus (the fleshy pad where your thumb meets your palm) of both parties will naturally press against the shot glass. Air your dirty laundry. Work it out. Apologize if needed. Once you have worked out your differences, anoint the third eye (center of the forehead) and the heart of the other party. Consider a circle, an infinity symbol, or a heart as the symbol to trace. Take the leftover bourbon and pour it out as a thank you to the elements.

> *How to apologize to someone:*
>
> - *Acknowledge wrongdoing. Ownership is important. "I'm sorry IF I hurt you" is not an apology. "I hurt you, and I'm sorry," is.*
>
> - *State how you hurt the other person (it shows that you know what you are apologizing for). "I made you feel bad when I . . . "*
>
> - *Explain what you plan to do to remedy the situation.*
>
> - *State how the behavior will not repeat. ". . . because (state reason)."*

Remember, apologies are no guarantee of forgiveness. The offended party doesn't owe you anything. Being forgiven is not conditional on apologizing. Apologizing is the first step if there is reconciliation, but not an automatic response (otherwise, it is meaningless).

Childbirth—To petition for a smooth delivery, during the final weeks of the pregnancy or before going to the birthing place, anoint the belly with a small amount of bourbon (or corn flour). For best results, set a custard cup of bourbon in the sun for the blessings of the elements. Use sacred symbols of protection for an added benefit (stars, equal-armed crosses, circles, spirals).

Releasing fear—Pour a shot of bourbon, whisper your concern over the rim of the glass, and drink. See that fear vanishing after urination.

> **Sober Substitution**: Place a teaspoon of corn flour in a custard cup, and whisper your anxiety over the flour. Take it outside and throw the meal into the air and let it drift on the breeze. See the fear dissipating.

Libation—Because corn is associated with nature, spirits, and the like, use bourbon as a ceremonial offering to your deity of choice if other offerings are unavailable.

Love—To bring love into your life, write a list of traits you want in a partner, whether platonic or romantic. Fold the piece of paper and place it in the bottom of a small pot. On top of the paper, place a handful of cornmeal (blessing) and fill with soil. Plant nine basil seeds (sacred to Aphrodite, associated with love), and water it. Place in a sunny window. Tend the basil plants as you would a relationship—talk to them, feed and water them. Your love will grow. If you don't have the time to spend on a potted plant, you cannot nurture a budding relationship. Make time for yourself and make time to nurture the people in your life. Use the basil in dishes that can be prepared for loved ones.

Ambition—We all need some encouragement from time to time. Take a handful of cornmeal and tell it what you want to accomplish. Cast it into the outside air or a fire to release the energy and set the intention in motion.

Feeding spirits—Spirit can have a negative connotation. In this instance, the land wights or spirits of place deserve the honor. They like cheap candy and cheap liquor. Pour out a shot or two for your land spirits and let them know you recognize them. Feeding house spirits cornmeal or bourbon can help save on last-minute repairs and keep disaster from your home.

Luck—To bring luck into the home, place a handful of cornmeal at each of the four corners of the house (feel free to add a pinch of ground clove for a luck boost), or anoint the windows with a drop of bourbon.

Relationship harmony—Grab a shot glass and a partner (or partners) and head outside. Face each other. Each person should fill the shot glass with bourbon, and make a wish for the other (or another) person. The shot is then poured on the ground to the spirits. Feel free to imbibe a shot if you do more than one round.

 Sober Substitution: Use popcorn kernels instead of alcohol. Pour the kernels into a pot and make popcorn to be enjoyed. Remember to set aside a serving of popcorn for the land spirits.

Releasing captives—In an old tome, I found a spell to release captives using corn, which can also be used to release unconscious thoughts. If those thoughts are unconscious, how do we put them into words to be released? Write yourself a letter. It can be addressed to anyone, really, but it isn't meant to be mailed. Get all your thoughts and feelings written down. Fold the paper into a small packet and pour in a few pinches of cornmeal or anoint with a high-proof bourbon like Knob Creek to light the paper in a fireproof container.

Releasing anxiety around social situations—Before leaving the house, anoint the top of each foot with bourbon in an equal-armed cross for stability.

Sober Substitution: Place a pinch of corn flour in the bottom of each shoe before heading out to social gatherings.

RECIPES

Old-Fashioned Witch

Tools

» Old-fashioned glass

Ingredients

» 1½ oz. bourbon (prosperity, fertility, prosperity, blessing)

» 1 oz. Amaretto (creativity, passion, love, opening the mind, relaxation)

» 1 tsp. superfine sugar

» 1 tsp. cold water

» A dash of orange bitters—see Chapter 7 to make your own!

» Orange peel (prosperity, abundance, affection, creativity, divination)

» Ice

Sprinkle the sugar in the bottom of an old-fashioned glass.

Add the orange bitters.

Place a teaspoon of water in the glass to marry the sugar and flavor.

Add ice to the glass.

Pour bourbon and Amaretto into the glass and swirl.

Express orange peel over the glass and use it as a garnish.

Drink while savoring the flavor and envisioning the outcome.

Stone Fruit Whiskey

Tools

» 1 quart jar with lid

Ingredients

» Whiskey of your choice

» Cherries, peaches, apricots, plums, and other stone fruits

» Optional: 1 vanilla bean

As the harvest period rolls along, save all the stones from your stone fruit. Whether pitting cherries or enjoying your first peach of the season, place all stones in the quart jar. Make sure the pits are covered with whiskey; as you add stones, add whiskey. By the time winter rolls around, it will be ready. The seeds add a woody and sweet flavor to the whiskey. It's nice for sipping as is, or for adding to cocktails.

CACHAÇA, RUM

Main Botanical: Sugarcane (Saccharum officinarum)

Botanical Family: Poaceae (grasses)

World Origin: New Guinea 6000 BCE

Part of Plant Used: Juice

Scent Description: Sweet—the first pressing is darker; the second is lighter, fresher

Scent Impact: N/A

MAGICAL CORRESPONDENCES

Element: Fire

Day: Friday

Magical Uses: Lightening mood, love, lust, sex, uplifting, preservation, recovery

Planet: Venus

Astrological Signs: Libra, Taurus

Suggested Crystal: Rose Quartz

Deity/Spirit: Venus

Warnings: None

HERBAL LORE AND USES

Sugarcane is one of humankind's first cultivated plants, going back eight thousand years. It is also the most produced in terms of weight annually. It can produce sweetener, building materials, paper, molasses, and eleven or more alcoholic beverages, plus ethanol for fuel and more. It has incredible versatility for biomass, too.

This member of the grass family is not only associated with fire because of its Venus rulership; fire is used in the harvesting of sugarcane as well. These canes can reach heights of twenty feet (six meters). The grasses provide shade for spiders, moles, voles, lizards, and snakes, and as such, it can be a dangerous proposition to harvest. The danger from small animals is less now with the practice of burning the sugarcane fields. The canes stay strong and withstand the heat of the flame, while the razor-sharp grass burns away and chases the wildlife to a safer area.

Like fruit that grows in bunches, the bottommost segment of this member of the grass family ripens first. Each section of the grass matures at its own pace, from the bottom up.

Sugar and other natural sweeteners have been used sympathetically to sweeten dispositions in folk magic for hundreds of years, if not longer. The long history of rum being used in magical applications should surprise no one. Grasses evolved more than fifty-five million years ago, and the canes have been useful since before recorded history.

Cachaça (pronounced *ka-SHAS-a*) is the national liquor of Brazil and the principal spirit of its national drink, the caipirinha, which loosely translates to "little peasant girl." It is made from fermented sugarcane juice, whereas rum is made, in most cases, from the molasses. Though Cachaça 51 is the brand most readily found in the United States, Brazil lists over a thousand producers of the spirit. It is made from the first pressing of the sugarcane, and this unrefined juice is distilled, but not aged in oak barrels like many other spirits. It has a flavor somewhere in between rum and tequila, with a bite. The caipirinha is more closely related to a mojito and is made with muddled lime and sugar. Cachaça is so renowned (and loved) there are urban legends of this high-proof spirit being used to fuel a Ford Fairlane. There may be some truth to it, as ethanol derived from sugarcane can be purchased at gas stations in Brazil.

Please note: Rum has religious uses for practitioners of the religions of the African Diaspora. Please use respectfully.

PRACTICAL USES

Antidepressant—Place a teaspoon of sugar in coffee or tea and visualize it brightening your day as you drink.

Love—Spread a teaspoon of sugar on a saucer. Trace a heart in the sugar while visualizing the impact of love, platonic, familial, or romantic. Send the energy into the sugar, and add it to your beverage, stir clockwise, and sip, continuing the visualization.

Lust—Mix the following ingredients in a glass bowl with a wooden spoon.

» 1 cup table sugar (lust)

» 1 oz. jojoba oil or sunflower oil (perseverance, solar blessings)

» 1 tbsp. brown sugar (sex magic)

» 4 drops tangerine essential oil—*Citrus reticulata* (confidence)

» 2 drops cardamom essential oil—*Elettaria cardamomum* (lust)

» 2 drops ylang-ylang essential oil—*Cananga odorata* (sensuality)

Use as an in-shower body scrub on chest, arms, and legs to invigorate, empower, and entice. As always, use caution in the shower with oils present.

Mood lifting—Fill a 2 ounce water bottle with 1 ounce light rum or cachaça, 12 drops tangerine oil (mood lifting), and 1 ounce water. Shake. Spritz around the home to brighten the mood. Beware of light-colored fabrics, as it may cause staining.

Justice/Just Judge—Take your court documents if you have any, and copy them. If courts aren't involved, write out the scenario in your own handwriting. Take the papers, fold as small as possible, and place in a small box. Place a tablespoon of brown sugar (it is flavored with molasses, so has extra sugary magic to it) inside the box. If you have access to dirt from a courthouse, put that in there, too. I take an apple and some water in a brown paper bag to the local courthouse and sit near the landscaping. I eat my apple and drink my water, and, as inconspicuously as possible, put a handful or two of the soil in my paper bag. When I'm done, I dispose of the core and go home with my Justice dirt in tow.

Caipirinha (Lusty Lady)

Tools

» Heavy-bottomed scotch glass

» Muddler

Ingredients

» 2 oz. Cachaça 51 (sex magic)

» 5 lime wedges (fidelity, healing)

» 2 tsp. turbinado sugar (lust)

» Ice

» Optional: strawberries (happiness)

Place the lime wedges, and strawberries if desired, in the bottom of a heavy-bottomed scotch glass.

Sprinkle in sugar and muddle until sugar is dissolved. Stir clockwise to grow thoughts of lust and sex. Add ice to the glass.

Pour cachaça into a glass and stir gently.

Enjoy while meditating on the outcome.

GIN

Main Botanical: Juniper (Juniperus communis)

Botanical Family: Cupressaceae

World Origin: North America (Utah), Europe, Asia

Part of Plant Used: Berries

Scent Description: Bright green, herbal, piney

Scent Impact: Encourages feelings of peace, love, and healing

MAGICAL CORRESPONDENCES

Element: Fire

Day: Sunday

Magical Uses: Anti-theft, protection (especially from hexes), libido, banishing negativity, love wishes

Planet: Sun

Astrological Sign: Aries

Suggested Crystal: Sunstone

Deity/Spirit: Ares

Warnings: Do not ingest juniper if pregnant or nursing. Avoid long-term use.

HERBAL LORE AND USES

One of the oldest magical incenses, juniper dates back to the Triassic period 250 million years ago. This fragrant shrub is incredibly versatile as a magical ally and a botanical spirit. This tree (or shrub, depending on the subspecies) is so old that it has the largest geographic range of any woody plant. It is found in North America, Europe, and Asia. Certain subspecies can live over two hundred years. Like many evergreens, the shrubs and trees are either male or female. The delicate pollen of a male plant can be carried on the wind, over a hundred miles away. Once pollinated, the berries take two to three years to mature. The juniper's signature berries are actually a kind of pinecone, with microscopic scales, so they appear as berries. Both terms are correct, though the term "berries" is more universally used.

Because of the unusual ripening habit and growth, the berries ripen a few times a year. So, rather than being farmed, juniper berries are commonly wild-crafted and sold to distillers and herb suppliers. Juniper wants to keep its fruit as long as possible, so all stages of ripeness cling to the plant.

Like absinthe, gin's signature flavors derive from a blend of botanicals. Sloe gin is the gin that derives additional flavor from sloe, the berries of the blackthorn (*Prunus spinosa*). Sloe gin enables banishing work, cleanses the aura of disharmony, strengthens protection, and also provides protection from negative ghosts.

Other botanicals included in gin are:

» Angelica (protection)

» Cardamom (confidence)

» Coriander (clairvoyance)

» Fennel (protection)

» Ginger (energizing)

» Grains of paradise (banishing)

» Lavender (harmony)

» Orris root (love)

Gin was already being distilled in the mid-1560s by the Dutch. When the English joined the fight against Spain, they discovered this delicious spirit and they readily enjoyed the liquor on the battlefield. Rather than being its own base spirit, think of gin as juniper-flavored vodka. There is also juniper brandy, popular in Eastern Europe, made by fermenting the juniper berries then distilling the ferment.

Juniper was burned in Ancient Greece to purify temples before ritual and worship because of its protective and purifying qualities. Juniper is planted by the entrances of properties and homes to guard against theft. The berries have been boiled in alcohol for magic involving libido and erectile dysfunction. The incense of the burning juniper is used to break hexes, increase psychic power, and protect people from accidents.

PRACTICAL USES

Talent—When learning a new skill, place a sprig of juniper in a pocket, or as close to your heart as you can, to ensure the knowledge roots in your heart.

Protection from accidents/harm—Anoint hands, heart, and feet with gin while envisioning yourself whole and protected.

> **Sober Substitution**: Take 2 ounces of rubbing alcohol and 5 drops of juniper essential oil (*Juniperus osteosperma*). Blend, bottle, and anoint as above.

Enabling action—Feeling stuck in the sand? Have a project to complete? Anoint the bottoms of the feet with gin.

> **Sober Substitution**: Use a sprig of juniper to brush away any negative attachments from the feet.

Protection from ghosts—Using gin or rubbing alcohol with a drop of juniper diluted therein, dip a juniper branch into the liquid and sprinkle over the exterior of the home, if possible. If in an apartment, use the outside edges of the interior. For added benefit use sloe gin, or place a sloe in the four corners of the home after a cleansing has been performed.

Banishing—Write the name of the person or habit to be banished on paper (preferably in ink). Include a one-word description of why you want them banished from your life. This step is important because it forms a concrete picture of your life without them in it, in your mind.

"Sally Jones, gossip." (No, I don't know anyone named Sally Jones/wink) This is all that is needed, but if you know biographical data like date, time, and place of birth, include it. This ensures that you are directing the energy toward the correct Sally Jones. Fold the paper and place it into a small dish like a custard cup. Pour an ounce of gin (or juniper-scented rubbing alcohol) into the dish, over the paper. If the gin starts to wash away the ink, even better. Leave in a rarely used corner, somewhere it won't be disturbed. Let the gin evaporate, and so will their influence on your life. Once the liquid has all evaporated and the paper is dry, burn the paper, bury it off of your property, or dispose of it away from your home.

Protection from anger—To protect yourself from your own anger, grab some cheap gin, a pitcher of water, and black food coloring. Pour an ounce of gin into a water glass. Sit with the glass and meditate on the things causing you anger, frustration, and other unwanted feelings. Anger can be fear projected outward. Think about whether there is something you fear causing this anger. Each time you think of a new angry subject, place a drop of black food coloring in the gin. Keep going until you run out of fear and anger. Take one finger and dip it into the black gin. Place a drop of the food-colored gin on the back of each hand. Sometimes our inner thoughts and feelings have external clues. Name the water in the pitcher with things that make your life better, even if you can only think of one thing at the moment. Take the water and rinse the black dots off the backs of your hands. Hold the glass of gin in your nondominant hand and the water in your dominant hand. Start slowly pouring the water into the gin glass. Notice how it dilutes the gin, lightening the color. Pour faster. Pour that water until there is only clear water in the glass and all the dark gin has been pushed out by the light of your water. Take a sip of the water from the now-clean glass and know you are whole, always. Even if it doesn't feel like it today. This will ground that feeling in the long term.

Sober Substitution: Add 3 drops juniper essential oil to a glass of water with the food coloring.

Note: If you feel like you need protection from someone else's anger, there are resources for you: domestic violence, including same-sex couples, teenagers, and more. You do not have to stay. Don't believe the threats; get help however you can. I have faith in you.

Protecting animal health/reversing ill health—Alcoholic beverages are not healthy for our animal friends. If you have a pet that is ill, to help speed their recovery, use a juniper branch over their energetic body (you don't have to touch them with it) to brush away the energy of illness from them.

Dreams—To fight night terrors and bring on beneficial dreams, anoint the base of the skull, temples, and third eye with gin (or witch hazel with a drop of juniper dissolved in it). Perform one-half hour before bed. For added benefit, use sloe gin.

Aura cleansing/spiritual transformation—Ignite incense charcoal (safely!) and place dried juniper (with or without berries) on the steadily burning charcoal. As it starts to smoke, scoop the smoke as you would water from a bucket, and "pour" the smoke from the fire over your head. Scoop more to direct over each arm and down your shoulders. Direct the smoke down your torso and each leg. See yourself full to bursting with light—light bright enough to burn away any attachments, illness, or sluggishness in your aura. It is done. Consider sealing the work by anointing forehead, heart, stomach, hands, and feet with gin.

Fertility/erectile dysfunction—Draw a warm bath (not too hot!), and grab salt (table or Epsom), gin (optional), juniper essential oil, a bowl, and a toothpick or wooden stir stick to mix with. Place 2 cups of salt in a glass or nonreactive bowl. Place 2 drops of juniper into the salt. Mix the salt and juniper. Add an ounce of gin if working with the spirit.

Mix. Add to the bathwater and mix with the warm water to dissolve. Note: Juniper is high in Alpha-pinene; 20–40 percent of the chemical makeup of the essential oil is a lot and can sensitize skin if too much is used. Bathwater will touch sensitive parts of the body, so less is more. If you over add, just add more salt to dilute. Step carefully into the bath, and as you submerge yourself into the bath, see the juniper permeating your system, pushing anything out of your body that no longer serves, so that it exits the bloodstream to the liver and kidneys, to be expelled from the body during urination. With your eyes closed visualize all systems of the body as a functioning whole that is empowered by your highest good. Clear them with your visualizations, one by one. Stay and meditate until the water cools. Rinse if desired. As you (gently) towel dry, enjoy the loving, comforting scent of juniper reminding you that you are a loving being.

Protection from hexes—Hang a bundle of juniper over the main entrance to the home.

Lighting the way—Burn juniper candles to guide a loved one home safely.

Past life—Burn juniper as an incense while meditating on your past, replaying your life in rewind. Keep going back, before the time of your birth. Allow visions of your most recent life to fill your vision.

Prosperity—Cleanse your wallet, bank statements, and any ledgers you use in the smoke of burning juniper leaves and berries.

Protection from theft—Make a magical pen. Take a 10 ml roller bottle (they now make gemstone rollerballs for 10 ml roller bottles!) and place a drop of juniper essential oil inside. Fill with the carrier of your choice. I suggest jojoba or fractionated coconut oil because of the extended shelf life. Cap with the rollerball and lid, and gently roll the sealed bottle between your hands to gently mix. Mark any items you fear being stolen, as long as oil won't damage the surface. If oil can damage the surface, anoint the index finger on your dominant hand and project your preferred symbol of protection onto the surface of the item. The juniper will be included in the intention.

RECIPES

Bad Boy Be Gone

Tools

- » Cocktail shaker
- » Martini glass

Ingredients

- » 1½ oz. gin (protection from ghosts)
- » 1½oz. apricot brandy (defense from evil, banishing distrust)
- » Juice from half a lemon (calming, clarity, love)
- » Cherry for garnish (happiness, love)
- » Ice

We all have someone in our past that reminds us of how nice things used to be. We are fighting the ghosts of our memories. Our memories lie to us. Things were never as rosy as our hormones want us to think they were. Don't text that someone. Banish them from your bedroom and your libido with this cocktail.

Place all ingredients minus the cherry into the cocktail shaker with ice. Empower the potion by shaking it as hard as you can, until frost forms on the metal of the cocktail shaker. Serve in a martini glass.

VODKA

Main Botanical: Potato (Solanum tuberosum)

Botanical Family: Solanaceae

World Origin: Peru (seven to ten thousand years ago)

Part of Plant Used: Root

Scent Description: Wet, earthy, mildly astringent

Scent Impact: N/A

MAGICAL CORRESPONDENCES

Element: Earth

Day: Monday

Magical Uses: Healing, comfort, protection (especially of public image), money, luck

Planet: Moon

Astrological Sign: Capricorn

Suggested Crystal: Howlite

Deity/Spirit: Hestia/Vesta

Warnings: Root is safe. Greens are toxic; do not ingest.

HERBAL LORE AND USES

This tuber has been cultivated for between seven and ten thousand years. Though it has a wide history and a tragic one due to the Irish Potato Famine, this root vegetable was discovered in the Andes mountains, and all varieties and cultivars have this single potato as their genetic mother.

Texts enumerating the ways potatoes were used as the first poppets have proven that this innocuous starch has a variety of uses. The eyes of the potato can be cut from it and used as eyes for magical purposes, to decorate a poppet, or to see into other places or realms.

Vodka today is commonly distilled from potatoes or grains, though some manufacturers like to incorporate fruits into their proprietary recipes. It originated in Russia and Poland. The name is the diminutive version of water (*voda*); the "ka" sound is a blend of the diminutive "k" and feminization "a." Since records are hard to find on the history of this spirit, it is hard to know exactly the time and place it was invented. The word vodka didn't appear in Russian dictionaries until the mid-1800s. Poland has records of vodka distilleries being in operation in 1784.

PRACTICAL USES

Protection—Place a splash of vodka into a shot glass or custard cup. Anoint your head, shoulders, hands, knees, and feet while seeing yourself whole, protected, and secure. Consider adding the visualization of a protective shielding around you. It can be an egg, a brick wall, anything that you can concretely picture in your mind, using as many senses as you can. If you use an egg, picture how it would look surrounding you. Imagine the texture of the interior and exterior. Is there a chalky smell associated with the eggshell, or does the shield block out smells? The more detail the better.

Prosperity—Take a dollar bill, or copy one side of a bill if you're more comfortable with that, and anoint the four corners of the bill with vodka. Place the bill in your wallet and don't spend it. It'll grow your prosperity as long as it is in place.

Protection of home—Buy the cheapest vodka you can find. It will likely be 80 proof; that's just fine for this. Go to the northeastern corner of your property. Pour out the vodka in splashes, anointing your property line with the vodka. Silently or aloud, ask the spirits of place to protect your home and all who dwell within it. Complete the boundary of your home. (Feel free to water it down if needed.)

Sober Substitution: You're going to make smashed potatoes to accompany dinner. Fill a cookpot halfway with cool water. Peel the number of potatoes needed and cut them into 1 inch cubes. Let sit for 30 minutes in the water. Pour off the starchy water into another container. Fill with clean, cool water, and cook 20 minutes on high until soft enough to be pierced with a fork. Strain water out, add butter, and mash with a wooden spoon until roughly mashed. Enjoy. Take the first pot of starchy water and pour it along the boundaries of your property to mark it as your own, and ground any negative influences that come your way.

Money—Under a waning moon, gather a large potato, a vegetable peeler, and a permanent marker. Write the source of money problems on the potato. Show the potato to the light of the moon and say, "I banish you (name the luck drain)." Peel the potato, starting with the offending word. Continue peeling until the potato is too small to safely continue to peel. Discard the potato peelings off of your property.

Healing—Draw a gingerbread man shape on a piece of heavy brown paper (paper grocery bags are perfect). It doesn't have to be great; no one will see it. Name it with the name of the friend who needs healing. Draw on the affected area, chest for a chest cold, arm for a broken arm, and so forth. Cut a potato in half, and, using the cut side, scrub away the illness, injury, and the like. Rinse the brown paper with (cheap) vodka until the paper looks illness free. Keep for a week to make sure the spell takes. Repeat if needed. Best done on a full moon or a Monday.

Luck—Rinse the bottom of your shoes with vodka so that, wherever you go today, you are blessed by the moon and with good luck. (I have also done this on the wheels of my wheelchair; both work.)

Guarding your public image—Write out any threats to your public image on paper. In a fireproof container, splash high-proof vodka onto the paper and carefully ignite. See the threats disappear.

> **Sober Substitution**: Write the threats to the public image on flash paper and ignite.

RECIPES

Blueberry Girl Banishing

Tools

- » 1 large mason jar
- » Muddler
- » Cheesecloth

Ingredients

- » ¾ cup of ripe blueberries (banishing, protection)
- » 16 oz. vodka (protection, healing, luck)

Place the blueberries in the mason jar, holding the image of the person or situation to be banished. Muddle the blueberries to release all of that beautiful juice and flavor. Feel free to sing while muddling; it'll add energy to your brew.

Pour the vodka into the mason jar, cap, and shake to infuse. Keep that image in your mind; you're imprinting your desire on the vodka.

Strain the blueberry pulp from the vodka with cheesecloth, and squeeze to get every last drop.

Store in the refrigerator for best flavor.

Pour a shot, say the name of the person or situation to be banished aloud, and drink! They'll be gone in twenty-four hours or the situation will quickly resolve.

Molotov Cocktail

Tools

- » 1 medium plate
- » 1 heavy-bottomed glass
- » Cocktail shaker

Ingredients

- » 4 oz. tomato juice (protection)
- » 2 oz. pepper vodka (banishing)
- » 2 tbsp. horseradish (banishing)
- » 2 tsp. Worcestershire sauce (banishing)
- » 2 tsp. A.1. Sauce (dissolving connections)
- » 2 tsp. celery salt plus extra for garnish (mental clarity)
- » 1 lime wedge (strength)
- » 1 tsp. ground black pepper (banishing)
- » ½ tsp. smoked paprika
- » Celery stalk for garnish

Place the extra celery salt on the plate.

Rub the rim of the glass with cut lime and roll the edge of the glass in the celery salt to coat.

Squeeze the lime into the cocktail shaker. Place spent wedge into the glass. Top with ice. Into the cocktail shaker, place pepper vodka, tomato juice, horseradish, sauces, and spices. Cap and shake vigorously. Strain into glass and add celery as garnish.

This is a banishing of the highest order. When a person or situation needs to be banished overnight, grab this peppery version of a Bloody Mary. Feel free to spice it up as *much* as you'd like. All peppers are banishing, so the spicier the better. Burn it down.

WINE

Main Botanical: Grape (Vitis vinifera)

Botanical Family: Vitaceae (part of the rose grouping)

World Origin: Turkey, Egypt

Part of Plant Used: Fruit

Scent Description: Bright, sweet, watery

Scent Impact: N/A

MAGICAL CORRESPONDENCES

Element: Water

Day: Monday

Magical Uses: Fertility, prosperity, devotional, money

Planet: Moon

Astrological Sign: Cancer

Suggested Crystal: Shiva lingam

Deity/Spirit: Bacchus

Warnings: Grapes are generally regarded as safe. For wine, talk to your doctor about risk factors.

HERBAL LORE AND USES

The cultivation of grapes began between six and eight thousand years ago. They have been used to make food, oil, drinks, and more, as well as having many uses in religious services. Grapeseed oil was used by ancient Greeks to anoint statues of the Greek gods and show worship and devotion. Christians use grapes in both wine (transubstantiation of wine into the blood of Christ) and, for those sects abstaining from alcohol, grape juice during the rite of Holy Communion. Catholics, in particular, use wine, with the more Protestant sects choosing to use blessed grape juice. Canon Law #924 says that wine must be used in Holy Communion and that the grapes used must be natural and free from corruption. (It is assumed here that corruption refers to rotten fruit, which could ruin the batch of wine.)

The world's oldest documented winery, found in Armenia, has been dated to 4000 BCE. Because of the long history of this plant, its fruit, and the drinks derived from it, it is an excellent choice to use for libations and spell work. The gods have a long history with it and recognize it. Where a modern energy drink would still have an impact, the wine carries with it all the energy of those who have libated wine before you.

PRACTICAL USES

Fertility—Take turns with your lover (or lovers) feeding each other green table grapes that have been blessed. (Blessing can be done by anyone; praying over them and anointing with wine or charged water are all suitable blessings.) Optional: drink wine and enjoy each other's company. The spirit of ecstasy is said to live in the grape and blesses all unions.

Prosperity—Print a copy of your recent bank statement or write an account balance on a piece of paper. Fold the paper and put it in a small bowl. Each day, pour a small amount of wine onto the paper to feed the spirit of your finances and watch your wealth grow. Best performed in the light of the Moon.

Devotional—To show devotion to a particular deity, leave glasses of wine in front of statues, photos, drawings, or other representations of Them.

Repeat every three days—pour out the wine, rinse the glass, and renew. Best done around festival dates.

Accolades—To receive recognition for your accomplishments, draw a medal for your achievement on paper. (This can be a circle on a Post-it; we aren't judging artistic talent.) Label the award with your name and why you have received it. Place it in a small bowl. Each day for 7 days, pour a small amount of wine and grapes into the bowl. After 7 days, feel free to compost the grapes. Your recognition will come within a lunar cycle.

Overcoming self-consciousness—On a night you aren't planning on leaving the house, pour yourself a glass of wine (or grape juice). For each sip, name something about yourself that you love, that you like, that you are good at. Keep going until you run out of wine. Optional: ask Hathor to renew your view of yourself as she renews the cosmos.

Inspiration—Leave a glass of wine or grape juice in the light of the moon for an hour. Visualize the light of the moon filling the chalice. Drink the liquid and know it has been blessed by the elements and allow yourself to draw your inspiration from its depths.

Love—Grab a bunch of red grapes and, optionally, the wine of your choice. Make a list of your ideal qualities in a lover, and after naming each one, pluck and eat a grape, taking into yourself your ideal partner's qualities. This will show the universe that you know your worth and the kind of love you deserve. Enjoy this time. You are amazing and anyone would be lucky to be with you. Know it, live it. You are a whole person, not a half. Go into your new relationship knowing how lucky you both are to have found each other.

Bishop (Get That Money)

Tools

- » Cocktail shaker
- » Wineglass

Ingredients

- » 4 oz. light, chilled, dry red wine (money, accolades, inspiration)
- » Juice of ½ a lemon (security, focus, purification)
- » Juice of ½ an orange (abundance, ambition, dreams)
- » ½ oz. simple syrup (mood elevating)
- » Ice

This recipe goes back to the 18th century and should be enjoyed, as everyone who has enjoyed it before you. Know that you are an empowered being, worthy of all you have worked so hard for. Place ice in a cocktail shaker with lemon juice, orange juice, and simple syrup. Shake vigorously. Pour into a chilled wineglass. Add chilled wine to the glass and stir gently. Enjoy while visualizing your successes coming to pass.

Don't be afraid to experiment!

Botanical Brews
in the Kitchen

With this book, finding your allies in the kitchen will become just a little easier. In this chapter, we will be discussing different nonalcoholic potions to create, how ingredients benefit our cooking, and how these ingredients can work together to attain your magical desires. We have already covered some of the tools that we might use to work our magic and how they correspond to magical tools with which you may already be familiar.

Why make magic in the kitchen? The foods we eat are not only integral to our survival, but are also the main component of bonding with friends and family. Doing magic with the ingredients for food preparation is one of the oldest forms of magic. In ancient Egypt, it was understood that, for beer brewing, a half-baked loaf of bread must be sacrificed to the brewing vat for fermentation to occur. Wine is one of the oldest fermented beverages because of the wild yeast strains living on the surface of the fruit. The ancients may not have known why things happened, and isn't that the definition of magic we get from Arthur C. Clarke?—"Magic's just science that we don't understand yet."

Here are some magical ingredients to get you going.

APPLE

Botanical Name: Malus domestica

Botanical Family: Rosaceae

World Origin: Tian Shan mountains in Central Asia

Part of Plant Used: Fruit

Scent Description: Bright, sweet, tangy

Scent Impact: N/A

Related spirits: Cider, cyser, calvados

MAGICAL CORRESPONDENCES

Element: Water

Day: Friday

Magical Uses: Love, healing, blessing, fertility, physical activities, consecration, offerings to the dead

Planet: Venus

Astrological Sign: Taurus

Suggested Crystal: Carnelian

Deity/Spirit: Idunna

Warnings: Fruit is generally regarded as safe; seeds are poisonous in large doses.

HERBAL LORE AND USES

"An apple a day keeps the doctor away" is a common saying, and people are giving this rosy fruit a chance to live up to its name. Over ninety-five million tons of apples are produced worldwide annually. This figure represents over 7,500 varietals for eating, pressing into cider, and cooking. Half of the production of this tonnage comes from China, where the apple originated.

This member of the rose family has a long association with Venusian traits, including reverence for the five-pointed star that is found within the fruit when cut length-wise. Venus is associated with the five-pointed star because of the path it traces in the night sky. Therefore, the apple is associated with all magic ruled by Venus: love, sex, healing, beauty, the arts, fertility, and more.

The science behind the construction and biological diversity is fascinating; the *original* apple is the *Malus sieversii* or the wild apple. This apple has been found from Kazakhstan to China. In studying the genome of the apple, the most captivating fact is that apples have fifty-seven thousand genes. Humans have thirty thousand genes. Apples have more genes than any plant studied to date. All to produce one of the most recognizable fruits on the planet.

Apples, sweetest to most tart

1 Fuji

2 Jonagold

3 Autumn Glory

4 Courtland

5 Granny Smith

PRACTICAL USES

Physical Action—Have a bodily labor that you're capable of doing, but lack the motivation? Grab an apple and dig in. Some peel their apples, your choice. The sugar present in the apple will give you just enough energy to overcome the gravity of the sofa. It will also last long enough for you to finish the job.

Fertility—Looking to conceive? Take a green apple and ask Aphrodite to bless your union with a child. Bury it at the foot of an apple tree. Best done under a full moon or on a Friday.

Blessing your garden—To have a fruitful harvest, grab some apple juice or cider. If you have a farmer's market or orchard nearby, make it as natural as you can access. (Optional: ask Demeter to bless your soil while holding the juice aloft.) Take a sip and pour the liquid over the garden beds as an offering. This is sympathetic magic of the highest order. My favorite illustration of sympathetic magic was an ancient grimoire, full of flowery language. There was a spell in this grimoire that consisted of pouring a bucket of water on the ground to illustrate what the field should look like after the rains have come.

Love—Grab the red apple of your choice, cut it lengthwise to expose the five-pointed star within, and cover both halves with cinnamon (love, lust, sex) and honey (love, sweetness, sex). Ask Venus to grant you the love you desire in your life. Recite the desired qualities for the person you seek.

Healing—Take ½ cup of apple cider vinegar and, working with the patient, a photo, or even a drawing of a stick figure, bathe the affected (external) area every day for a week. Start on the full moon if possible, or a Sunday.

Asserting yourself—Learning to stand up for yourself can be so hard, especially if you have experienced traumatic or abusive relationships (familial, platonic, or romantic). Take ½ cup of apple cider vinegar and an optional three drops of lavender (*Lavandula angustifolia*) essential oil to relieve the weight of secrets and anything unsaid, and stir. With hands or cloth, anoint from throat to heart in a sweeping motion, and then from heart to throat. You are reminding your energetic body as well as the physical body that these two should be on speaking terms. Do this every day for a week. Feel free to extend it to a lunar cycle.

Contentment—On a Friday, gather a lovely, red, sweet apple and the honey of your choice. Three hours after sundown, put on something that makes you feel secure, happy, sexy, or right about yourself. Cut your beautiful apple into thin slices and set the seeds aside. Drizzle honey over the apple slices, take them somewhere comfortable to sit, and think of yourself as an ancient royal, reclining on a chaise lounge. Imagine the universe has laid out a banquet of infinite wishes. Think of what would make you happy, and for each dream you'd make, eat an apple slice until the bowl is empty. Optional: burn a red candle anointed with apple cider vinegar while you ruminate.

Beauty—Make your own apple cider vinegar toner.

RECIPES

Apple Cider Vinegar Toner

Tools

- » Clean bottle

Ingredients

- » 8 oz. water (cleansing, connection)
- » 3 tbsp. apple cider vinegar (healing, beauty, sexual attraction)
- » 1 tsp. chamomile hydrosol or 1 tsp. dried chamomile flowers (purification, aura balance, soothing skin)
- » 1 tsp. witch hazel—for oily skin only; it will dry skin (antianxiety, uncrossing, heart-healing)
- » 3 drops lavender essential oil—*Lavandula angustifolia* (protection, balance, gentleness)

Pour the vinegar into a clean bottle. Add the lavender essential oil. Cap and shake the bottle. Take the lid off and add the chamomile, witch hazel, and water. Replace the top and give another shake. Apply a small amount of toner to a clean cloth and gently wipe over the face.

With a clean face and a winning smile, tell yourself things you love about you. Practice makes perfect, so do this every morning. (Discontinue if irritation occurs.)

Birth—For a smooth delivery, cut an apple in half lengthwise and anoint with sunflower oil or apricot kernel oil. Leave as an offering under a tree or near your front door.

Blessing alcoholic beverages—For the home brewers out there, place 1 teaspoon of apple cider in ½ cup of apple cider vinegar. Add to a spray bottle and fill with water. Spritz over bottled beverages to add the blessings of Diana, Aphrodite, or Venus.

Nemoralia—The feast of Diana is traditionally August 13–15, and live branches bearing young apples were turned into torches and carried to the festival at Lake Nemi in her honor. She is the protectress of the wild, guardian of women in childbirth and young children. Her worship extends to this day with many modern adherents. Apples are a fitting offering for this night, as are bread and cookies shaped to resemble body parts that need healing, as well as the dedication of statues in Her honor. Some also offer garlic to Hecate during this time.

Blessing apple trees—Midsummer fires are also used to bless apple trees. The smoke warms the air, helps prevent mildew in humid regions, and helps drive away insects that could prey on the apples during this vulnerable time of year.

Binding—To bind someone from harming you, place their name, any biographical data you know (birthdate and the like) on a piece of paper. Include a photo if you have one (thanks to social media). Place it in a jar; an old pickle jar is perfect. Fill with apple cider vinegar, and cap. Their influence on your life will disappear. Remember, binding and banishing are two different things. Don't bind someone if you mean to banish them. Binding creates an energetic link to the person, tying them to you. Don't give them more energy than they deserve. If someone is worth binding, consider whether banishment might not be more appropriate. Rather than attempting to bind a criminal, thereby preventing them from further harmful behavior, see them getting caught and punished instead.

Clearing mental blocks—Place a teaspoon of apple cider vinegar into a glass of water. See that water washing away any mental blocks in your path. It works exceptionally well for executive dysfunction blocks. Drink the water.

Altar consecration—Grab a large spray bottle, add ½ cup of apple cider vinegar and 9 drops of frankincense essential oil, and fill with water. Spray over your altar space, and wipe down the surface. (Make sure it is dry; we don't want to damage the surface.) The altar is now clean both physically and energetically. Proceed with any consecration traditional to your belief, if needed.

Honor the dead—Slice an apple into sections, sprinkle cinnamon for affection, and drizzle with honey for love. Name the apples for your loved one. Leave these on your altar, or distribute outside. Since apples are found on most continents, they are very wildlife-friendly, so if they help themselves, great!

Decisions about relationships—Venusian associations with apples make them an excellent divination tool for love. As children, we grasp the stem of an apple and spin, calling letters as we go to discover the first letter in the name of our true love. To answer a yes/no question about your love life, using a paring knife, carefully peel the apple in a spiral. If the peel breaks, the answer is no. If you can complete the peel, throw it over your shoulder and read how the skin lands. If it forms a spiral or circle, the answer is yes. If it falls in a straight line, the answer is no.

Resisting desires—Shame is an overused disciplinary tool. Shame over our bodies, our love lives, or our ethical choices have no place here. Save embarrassment for things that matter. Are you the best person you can be? Do you help those in need? Do you show love and compassion to those around you? Wonderful. If you need to resist some temptation, dip apple slices in apple cider vinegar and remind yourself why you are avoiding it. If you are avoiding unnecessary spending to save for a vacation, say it. Telling yourself the right reasons for avoiding certain behaviors is beneficial for reinforcing your will. It also works for bad habits. "Texting and driving is dangerous and could hurt someone." When you start to engage in the pattern, you'll remember the ritual. Apple is associated with self-discipline to help keep you on track.

Sleep charm—Place the seeds from one apple in a small cotton bag and put it inside your pillowcase to draw sleep to you.

Defense against evil—Take two apples and cut length-wise. You should have four stars of Venus. Place each on a saucer or paper plate and put them outside the four corners of your home. On top of each star, set a bay leaf over the seeds to block negativity. If inside an apartment, make sure to place them where pets won't find them, as apple seeds can be harmful. Leave in place for a week before renewing or adding other protective measures. Compost the old apples. If outside, bring the plates in after a week.

Faith—To renew your belief in the divine or yourself, anoint a white or yellow taper in apple-scented oil or apple cider vinegar, and burn. Best done on a Friday.

Celebrity, recognition, success—For fame or attention, bury a golden apple under an apple tree and ask Aphrodite to bless you with renown.

Friendship/harmony—To repair a damaged friendship (after apologies and amends are accepted), cut open an apple (preferably red). On a small piece of paper, write your name, fold in half, and write the other person's name so that they touch when folded. Place inside the apple and bury on your property, if possible. If you have a patio instead of a yard, place it inside a planter. Plant something happy and loving in the pot (suggestions include tomatoes and strawberries). The apple will fertilize the living plant, and your quarrel will resolve itself. If amends are not accepted, wish them well and move on.

Initiation/dedication—For those undergoing an initiation, cider or apple juice is an attractive choice. "The blessings of Venus upon you. May the fruit of the goddess open the way for your new life's work. Blessed be the work, blessed be the witch."

Security—After cleansing the home, anoint the exterior doors, windows, backs of mirrors, and the main water and power spots in the house with apple cider or juice to keep your home protected and safe.

RECIPES

Mabon Flavored Sangria

Tools

> » Knife
> » Large pitcher or punch bowl

Ingredients

> » ½ gallon apple cider
> » 2-liter bottle of lemon seltzer water
> » 1 Jonagold, Gala, or Fuji apple (physical action, clear mental blocks)
> » 1 Granny Smith apple (strength, protection, consecration)
> » 1 pear (comfort, love, unions)
> » 1 orange (prosperity, strength, happiness)
> » 1 pomegranate (work/life balance, blessings, hope)

Wash the fruit thoroughly; grocery store apples are often waxed to preserve them for the long road from orchard to your home. Roughly chop apples and pear, and slice the orange. To peel the pomegranate, on the top side of the fruit (the part with the flower petal top), carve a pentagon and lift off the lid of the rind. Along the white seams between the fruit, carefully slice down towards the bottom. Fan out the segments of the fruit and easily remove them. Place all fruit into a large pitcher or punch bowl. Pour seltzer water into the container, and top with apple cider. Since the seltzer is lighter than the cider, it will mix better this way.

Chill and enjoy it!

BLACKTHORN SLOE

Botanical Name: Prunus spinosa

Botanical Family: Rosaceae

World Origin: Western Europe

Part of Plant Used: Fruit

Scent Description: Dark, woody, sweet

Scent Impact: N/A

Related spirits: Sloe gin

MAGICAL CORRESPONDENCES

Element: Water

Day: Friday

Magical Uses: Banishing, fidelity, justice, protection

Planet: Venus

Astrological Sign: Taurus

Suggested Crystal: Staurolite

Deity/Spirit: The Morrigan

Warnings: Fruit is generally regarded as safe; seeds are poisonous in large doses.

HERBAL LORE AND USES

This tree can be trained as a shrub, or grow to a height of fifteen feet (five meters). The name comes from the darkly colored bark and the thorny surface of its bark. Whitethorn is also closely allied. Blackthorns were used as boundary plants in western Europe, allowing for the tree to be trained down towards the ground as a living fence. Blackthorn thorns can break off in the skin and cause an infection, so they make a strong deterrent, as well as a strong fence to keep domesticated animals inside. The flowers that produce sloe fruit strongly resemble those of cherry blossoms, as they are a part of the same family and genus. The blackthorn has a smooth bark similar to a cherry, between the thorns. Because of the density of this wood, compared to its light weight, it makes a perfect walking stick, defensive tool, or, as they have in Ireland, something that does both, a shillelagh. Because these trees are found in Ireland, England, and Western Asia, it is rare to find sloe in the United States, but they can be used magically in the gin. With the advent of the Internet, the fruit can also be procured dried from specialty shops online, including specialty brewer's supplies, as sloe is also used to fake a port wine or add texture to a true port.

PRACTICAL USES

Banishing—Write out the person, people, or situation in need of banishing on a piece of paper, place 3 sloes in the center of the paper, and cast into a swiftly moving body of water. (Fruit and paper will rapidly decompose, posing no threat to land or wildlife.)

Destiny, fate—Need a sign from the universe, an empowering arrow to show you the way? Anoint a yellow candle with sloe oil—place 3 sloe berries into a 10 ml roller bottle, fill with carrier oil, add optional essential oil (rosemary is a good choice), and keep in a dark place for 3 weeks before using. Burn the anointed candle on a Wednesday.

Evil—To banish evil from your home, cleanse the home in the manner you deem appropriate. Directly afterwards, place a sloe in the corners of each room in your home. Optional: splash sloe gin on the doorstep.

Fidelity—To keep a lover faithful, anoint 1 candle that represents you, and 1 for your lover, with sloe gin and bind the 2 candles together with natural cotton twine. Place the bound candles into a fireproof container, like a cauldron filled with sand, and burn them on a Friday.

Sober Substitution: Replace sloe gin with sloe oil.

Disharmony—Blackthorn is hard to come by in the United States. If you are lucky enough to grow it yourself, take a piece of a young branch and use it to energetically sweep the house, allowing the thorns to pick up any lingering irritants or problems. Take the branch outside and cleanse it off of the property. Alternatively: anoint a ritual broom with sloe gin or sloe oil and charge it to sweep away disharmony.

Hexing—It is not our job to heal our abusers. If the time has come for an abuser to reap what she has sown, anoint a white candle with sloe oil and set it in front of a small mirror. A compact is fine, as is the bathroom mirror, providing it won't be disturbed. Best done on a Saturday (endings) or in the dark of the moon (banishing).

Illness—To banish illness, make yourself a Sloe Gin Hot Toddy and sip while under a massive pile of blankets. If you don't have sloe gin, substitute elderberry tincture.

Sloe Gin Hot Toddy

Tools

» Mug

Ingredients

» 1½ oz. whiskey (healing, protection, vitality)

» 1 cup hot water

» ½ oz. sloe gin (banishing, illness, protection)

» ½ oz. lemon juice (clarity, purification, banishing fatigue)

» 1 tbsp. honey (orange blossom preferred)

» Lemon wedge for garnish (healing, luck, relieving stress)

Pour ingredients into a warm mug and garnish with lemon or cinnamon stick.

Sip slowly.

Independence—When it's time to declare your independence from a person, place or situation, grab a red candle (ambition) and anoint it with sloe gin or sloe oil. Write "Freedom" on the side of the candle and burn it on a Tuesday (victory).

Protecting Children—The fierce thorns of a blackthorn are so good at their job, they not only draw blood when mishandled, they will poison you too. Much like parents protecting their young, blackthorn has many tricks up its sleeve. Grab a wreath of barley (healing, protect children, sacred) or wheat (advice, blessing, life, luck) from the craft store (or make one yourself, you crafty devil), and find a photo of your children (grandchildren, nieces and nephews, and so forth). Lay out newspaper to keep any oil or liquid from staining your work surface. Grab a small paintbrush, a custard cup, and newspaper. Place a small amount of sloe gin or sloe oil in the custard cup. Take the brush and barely dip the bristles into the liquid before brushing lightly over the surface of the wreath. Allow it to dry fully before affixing the photos of children to be protected in the center of the wreath. Tip: if the center hole for the wreath is too large, consider adding dried or silk flowers to the wreath to make a smaller opening.

Luck—Place 3 dried blackthorn sloes in a green or gold pouch. Carry the pouch on your nondominant side to draw luck to you. Add a gold candle anointed with sloe and burn on a Sunday.

Justice—Both the wood and the fruit of *P. spinosa* carry the weight of justice. To bring justice to someone's door, grab a white candle (purity of intent), a pinch of dirt from the local courthouse, a candleholder, and your sloe gin or oil. Place your (clean) candleholder in front of you on your work surface. Take your candle and carve the word "justice" into it. (A ball point pen will work just fine, but a candle scribe can be dedicated to the task.) Anoint the candle with your liquid sloe of choice. Place a pinch of courthouse dirt in the bottom of the candleholder, and place the candle on top, securely in the candleholder. Burn the candle on a Saturday to make sure the person can't hurt anyone else.

Negativity—To keep negativity from the home, light incense charcoal and burn small chips of cherry bark—first cousins to the blackthorn—to cleanse the home of negativity. Once the home has been cleansed, anoint all doors and windows with the protective symbol of your choice—equal-armed cross, circle, spiral, and the like—to seal the house from it returning. Renew seasonally.

Ending problems—A quick and easy way to banish specific problems (even problem people) is to speak it out and pass it out. Name the issue over the rim of a shot glass of sloe gin, and drink. The situation will soon end.

Protection—If you don't live in an area where blackthorn is prevalent, buy an ounce or two of sloe berries. Boil a gallon of water. Place the berries into the bottom of a five-gallon bucket, and carefully pour the boiling water over the berries. Allow them to steep for 10 minutes. Add another gallon or two of tap water to cool the blackthorn tea you've just made. Grab a small cup and head outside. Start in the northeast corner of your property and pour blackthorn tea all the way around your property line. Envision a powerful blackthorn fence growing up across the land, protecting all who reside inside. Alternatively: Grab a small wooden box, a handful of craft mirrors, silver paint, an aerial image of your property line (even if it is just the shape of your land), and a small photo of the occupants. Paint the small wooden box silver. Glue the mirrors to the exterior of the box, even if they only fit on the top and bottom. Place the printout of your home's parcel (even if you trace it onto a sticky note) inside the box. Add photos of residents if you have them and a handful of sloe berries. Charge under the light of the full moon.

Purification—Grab the roller bottle of sloe oil or a few drops of sloe gin. Sit in sacred space. Center your breath. Anoint your head, throat, heart, knees, and feet. Prayers at this time are appropriate if desired, not required.

Tina Collins (Happy Juice)

The Collins family is pretty extensive. Tom Collins is a gin-based drink. Juan Collins has a tequila base, while Ivan Collins has vodka, and the John Collins contains bourbon. Tina Collins uses sloe gin.

Tools

> » Tall glass

Ingredients

> » 1½ oz. sloe gin (luck, destiny, magic, protection)
> » ¾ oz. oleosaccharum—for more on what this is and how to make it, check out Chapter 8 (luck, prosperity)

- » ¾ oz. lemon juice—alternatively squeeze half a lemon, or a whole one, if it's small (calming, love, increasing power of a spell)
- » 1 twist of lemon peel for garnish (abundance, blessings, energy)
- » 3 dashes orange bitters (protection)
- » Sparkling water
- » Ice

Pour the sloe gin into a tall glass, add oleosaccharum, and stir. Add the lemon juice and bitters. Add ice and sparkling water. Express lemon peel over the rim of the glass and garnish. Sip while remembering happy times, or dream about joys to come.

CHERRY

Main Botanical: Prunus var. (principal variety P. avium)

Botanical Family: Rosaceae

World Origin: Turkey, Europe (digs have shown cherries in England from 2077 BCE)

Part of Plant Used: Fruit

Scent Description: Tart or sweet, musky, juicy

Scent Impact: N/A

MAGICAL CORRESPONDENCES

Element: Water

Day: Friday

Magical Uses: Attraction, balance, peace, victory

Planet: Venus

Astrological Sign: Taurus

Suggested Crystal: Venus jasper

Deity/Spirit: Astarte

Warnings: Fruit is generally regarded as safe; seeds can be toxic.

HERBAL LORE AND USES

This compact and sweet member of the rose family is widely varied. The genus Prunus has over 430 species, and those species are responsible for thousands of varieties each. Also, in the Prunus genus, we find plums, apricots, almonds, and even a few evergreens. Unlike the fruits in the citrus family, all of the stone fruits are descended from a single ancestor. Bronze Age archeology has found many examples of the tree being used two thousand-plus years before the common era. By 800 BCE, the tree was being cultivated in China. The sap from sweet and tart cherries was chewed before the advent of chewing gum.

Magically, its lineage from the rose family means that it is closely aligned with roses and other stone fruits, including blackthorn, nectarines, and almonds. If you have need of anything relating to beauty, the arts, luxury items, and the like, cherries are a great option, and they are linked medically with anti-inflammatory properties.

PRACTICAL USES

Attraction—To express attraction, grab a bag of ripe, sweet cherries, and share them with your intended. This works best on a Friday or during a full moon, perhaps after a Friday night date or coffee. Add a coffee bean to your pocket for added success in love affairs.

Awakenings—Spiritual awakenings are incredible; the whole world is before you. The air smells sweeter, colors are brighter, and you feel like you could take on the planet. To nurture that feeling, or to awaken yourself to new experiences, dine on a bowl of cherries, charged in the moonlight. If you can do this in the waxing moonlight, even better. Whether the light is streaming in through the window or you are outside, let the cool, nurturing feelings permeate your skin and fill you with wonder.

Balance—Pour a glass of cherry juice or cherry cider, raise energy within your palms, and push the feeling of balance into the juice. Drink while picturing what a more balanced life will look like.

Beautiful spirit—This potion takes a minute to put together, but the effects are long-lasting, inside and out.

Tools

> » Clean 10 oz. bottle—glass or number one plastic

Ingredients

> » 8 oz. water
>
> » 3 tbsp. cherry juice (beauty in spirit, peace, compassion)
>
> » 2 tbsp. apple cider vinegar (physical action, happiness, blessing)
>
> » 3 drops lavender essential oil—*Lavandula angustifolia* (peace, stimulating love, strength)

Add the apple cider vinegar to bottle. Add the lavender essential oil and swirl to mix. Add the cherry juice to the lavender vinegar. Top with 8 ounces of cool water. Use as daily toner with affirmations about your spirit and who you are as a person. "I am strong; I am thoughtful. I am always there for my friends."

Cheer/happy mood—Toast yourself with cherry juice or cherry cider. Leave the bottle of cider in a sunny window for an hour to charge before drinking. Pour it into a fancy glass if you have something you like. Picture the happiest moment you can recall up to that moment. Channel that feeling into the palms of your hands, and pick up the glass. Pour the happiness into that juice and allow it to imbue the drink with all the goodness you can muster. The cherries will do the rest, multiplying it magically. Drink, and feel the joy saturating every cell in your body.

Compassion—Grab a bowl of cherries and another bowl for the stones. Name the person you need to have compassion for, aloud (even if that person is you). Start naming things that you like about that person. I know this can be hard; I've been there. Place each pit into the separate bowl as you eat the cherries. When you have run out of things to say and cherries to eat, take the stones outside and place them in soil. Whether you cover them with earth in the garden or put them in landscaping planters on the street, let them touch the ground. The goal isn't to grow a cherry tree, just to ground those feelings in the real world. Each time you walk past that spot, you will remember the sweetness of the cherries and the exercise of trying to find things we enjoy about people we don't always like. It will reinforce the working and re-energize your magic.

Creativity—Collect cherry stones as you enjoy cherries. Let them dry on a paper plate (in a well-ventilated area to prevent mold). Once you have a handful or more, start strategically placing them around your creative spaces. Place a handful of them in the jar where your paintbrushes live. Tuck one or two in the bag with your photography gear. Iinsert a stone or two with pencils, pens, or charcoals. Allow these creative energies to bless your creative endeavors.

Deceit—If you're worried that someone has pulled the wool over your eyes, grab a white candle and carve one word to sum up the issue, "money," "love," or the like. Cut a cherry in half and rub it on the candle. Burn on a Sunday to reveal the truth. Burn on a Saturday to end the lies.

Divination—For a simple yes/no divination with cherries, hold a bag of lovely, ripe cherries and ask a question. Reach into the bag with your eyes closed and grab a handful. An even number of cherries grabbed is a yes, and an odd number of cherries is a no. Eat the cherries to cement the answer into reality. Put the cherries back and come back for a snack later if you'd rather not add any energy to that outcome.

Divine happiness—To receive blessings from the divine in your happiness, light a candle for the deity in question, and give them an offering of cherries. Leave them for three days before composting. If your wish is to be granted, it will be in the next seven days. Repeat if desired. "Sometimes, it isn't our work to do." —H. Byron Ballard

Harmony—If possible on a Friday, instill peace between people and allow harmony to reign again. Write both names on two separate pieces of paper. Use more papers if additional people are involved. If the people are teammates on the job or in an organization, list the place rather than all the names individually. Place a handful of cherries in a small jar (pickle jars are perfect for this), along with the names of the involved parties. Sprinkle sugar, honey, molasses, or any natural sweetener into the jar. Put the lid on the jar, and shake it with all your might. You're powering up the jar with all that energy. Optional: feel free to add sweetener and shake again, every day for a week. Let peace reign supreme.

Love—Grab a bag of cherries, a small bowl for stones, a candle (red, pink, or lavender), a candleholder, and a bowl in which the candleholder will fit. Bless your supplies. Fridays are traditionally date night, both because of the start of the traditional weekend and because Friday is ruled by Venus and is ideal for love, lust, sex, and beauty. For each trait you'd like an ideal partner to have, name it, eat a cherry, and place the stone in the small bowl. Repeat until you have built the ideal partner. Then take your candle, and carve the word "love" onto the surface. Pens work for this, as well as a nail or a screw; just be careful. Optional: anoint with cherry juice. Place the candle in the candleholder, and place the candleholder in the bowl. Around the candleholder, inside the bowl, pour the cherry stones to draw the ideal lover with all the traits you named. Light the candle, add words of power if you so desire, and allow the candle to burn out.

Memorial—Cherries carry the energy of death and rebirth, so they make a fitting memorial for a loved one who has crossed the veil. Their blooms remind us of the happy times and the fruit, the sweetness of life. If you don't have a property of your own, call the local library or park and ask if you can donate a tree for a memorial.

Victory—To accomplish something for which you cannot fail, cast cherry stones into a fire outside after blessing them with your intent and telling them how you intend to accomplish the feat.

Cherry tip: Most kitchen shops will carry a cherry pitter. They screw onto a small jar. Just place a cherry on the hole, and a small plunger pushes out the stone and keeps the fruit. It's quick and less risky than cutting stones out of cherries.

RECIPES

Mood-Lifting Maraschino Mash

Tools

» Large pitcher

Ingredients

» 3 cups sparkling water (cherry-flavored optional)

» 1 cup tart cherries—without stones; frozen is fine (peace, balance, compassion)

» 1 cup cherry juice (good cheer, happiness, harmony)

» 3 tbsp. superfine sugar (love, healing)

» 1 lime, juiced (friendship, focus, higher self)

» 1 handful mint sprigs (action, alertness, antidepressant)

Add the cherries to a large pitcher. Sprinkle the superfine sugar over the cherries and stir the cherries to release the juice and dissolve the sugar.

Pinch 4–5 pieces of mint from the bunch for garnish. Take the rest of the mint and slap it on the counter three or four times. This bruises the leaves and releases the flavor without muddling, which would release chlorophyll and muddy our drink. Place the bunch in the pitcher. Juice the lime if you haven't already done so. Place the halves of lime in the pitcher, and add the lime juice and cherry juice. Stir. Top with the sparkling water and stir gently. Chill 30 minutes and serve with a mint garnish.

LIME

Botanical Name: Citrus × latifolia, Citrus × aurantiifolia, others

Botanical Family: Rutaceae

World Origin: Iran (primary production), South Asia (origin)

Part of Plant Used: Fruit, zest

Scent Description: Bright, green, sweet, tangy

Scent Impact: Uplifting, invigorating

MAGICAL CORRESPONDENCES

Element: Fire

Day: Sunday

Magical Uses: Fidelity, healing, focus, friendship

Planet: Sun

Astrological Sign: Leo

Suggested Crystal: Yellow calcite

Deity/Spirit: Isis

Warnings: Generally regarded as safe.

HERBAL LORE AND USES

The lime, as with all citrus fruits, has its origins in South Asia. Lime is a hybrid of the mandarin orange and pomelo, with some back-sweeting (hybridizing the resulting offspring with mandarin for additional sweetness). Because these hybrids don't have the history that some plants do, in areas where the old grimoires were written, it is important to note that these offspring, or hybrids, carry the magical lineage of both of their parents. Since lime has more of the mandarin in its genetic makeup, its magical associations will follow that of the orange. Lemons, however, carry more of the pomelo genetic makeup, so it will follow the magical lineage of the pomelo associations. For more on lemon's magical lineage see my previous book *Blackthorn's Botanical Magic*.

PRACTICAL USES

Antidepressant—Lime is such an uplifting scent that it is easy to work with magically for alleviating the blues. Make yourself some lime-aid (even better than lemonade). Inhaling the lime scent as you juice the lime and zest the peel will be an uplifting experience. (See Chapter 7 on making limoncello with the lime zest.)

Make simple syrup using 1 cup water to one cup sugar, so there is no sugar sludge at the bottom of the pitcher. Heat water on the stove to boiling, turn off the heat and whisk in the sugar until the liquid is clear.

Zest the limes, and set aside zest for limoncello. Juice limes. Six or seven limes may be needed for one cup of juice. Late season limes will have more juice and a sweeter flavor than early season crops.

Add the lime juice and simple syrup to a large pitcher. Add 2 cups of water to the pitcher and stir. Give a test sip, as it might be too sweet. Add water until it gains the proper sweetness for you.

Tip: Stir with intent—clockwise to imbue the drink with happiness, using the spoon as your wand.

Note: Aromatherapy and magic are no replacement for talk therapy and medical intervention if needed. Both science and magic are complementary to the end goal of good health.

Fidelity—Take a teaspoon of lime zest, add it to a 10 ml roller bottle, and fill with jojoba oil or fractionated coconut oil. Allow to sit for 6–8 weeks and infuse in a warm room. You now have a magical pen with which to work any lime magic you wish. For fidelity in a relationship, draw a symbol that represents fidelity to you on the surface of a lavender or pink candle. Burn on a Friday to encourage loving feelings. Burn on a Saturday if you suspect infidelity and want it to end.

Friendship—To draw friendship to you, write "the right friend, right now" on a piece of paper, place a pinch of lime zest in the center of the paper, and fold. Place another pinch of lime zest in the bottom of a candleholder. Grab a yellow candle and write "friendship" on it and place it in the holder on top of the zest. Burn on a Wednesday to find your new friend.

Luck—To uplift your luck, write "my luck" on a piece of paper and place it in a jar. Then mix the peel from 2 limes with a cup of sugar in a bowl. Leave it on the counter where it won't be disturbed for 3 days. When you come back, it'll be a sweet, green, oily sugar that smells strongly of lime. Take a teaspoon a day and add it to the jar with your name. Each day, put the lid on the jar and burn a candle over it to empower it. Repeat for 1 week. (This oil sugar is called oleosaccharum, and is an old-fashioned punch ingredient. It pulls all of the available oil out of the peel and is much more flavorful than the zest. See Chapter 8 for more information.)

Hex breaking—Grab a pack of straight pins, a lime, paper, pen, and a knife, as well as black cotton fabric or black tissue paper. Cut the lime in half. Write the nature of the hex or the name of the person you believe responsible for the hex. This won't harm the person, but if you think things are hinky enough for someone to have put a hex on you, you don't need that person in your life. This will send them on their way. With the source of the hex on paper, place the paper in between the two halves of the lime. Stick the straight pins around the edge to hold the two halves together. (Careful, those little buggers hurt when you stab yourself doing this. Ask me how I know.) When the lime halves are as secure as they're going to get, wrap them in the black cloth or paper. Dig a hole in your yard (not in the garden; again, you don't want to find those pins with your fingers while digging in the garden next season). Cover the packet with dirt. The acid in the lime will dissolve the hex and the situation that led to it in the first place.

Stimulation—Herbs, plants, flowers, and fruit that have the power to stimulate the mind or body have the ability to boost your magic. The great thing about citrus fruits is the amount of oil contained in the skin, which means that all of the power they store in those nodules is available for magical purposes. Just add a bit of zest to your pouch, bag, jar, or candle, and you have the power of the whole lime. That leaves the rest of the fruit for making drinks with, flavoring your favorite food, and more. Way to stretch those dollars, fruit!

Strength—Not only does lime add mental stimulation to obstacles, allowing you to think your way out of a jam in a hurry, but magically it adds strength as well. Do you fear you lack the strength to accomplish a goal or have a difficult discussion with someone you care about? Lime is your cheerleader, goaltender, and more. Add a teaspoon of fresh lime zest any time you need a little extra strength, or your magic does.

Psychic talents/higher self—The scent of lime aromatically raises your energy, thoughts, and feelings to a higher plane/state of being. This is to say, lime can put you in tune with your other senses. Before intuitive readings for my clients, I take some slow, even breaths of lime essential oil to help me get out of my day-to-day brain and into the mindset of a professional reader, engaging with my third eye and other senses.

Tangerine/mandarin, lemon verbena, or lemon can help with this as well if lime isn't your favorite.

> *After my readings have finished for the day, I'll repeat the process with an earthy, grounding oil, like patchouli or vetiver, to ground my energy so I don't wind up with a psychic headache. If I haven't appropriately grounded or have done too many readings, my third eye feels like a sock full of hot nickels. Immediate grounding, like eating food or drinking some water or juice to bring me back to reality, is a must.*

Focus—Have an essential task to finish, and just can't get your figurative cats in a row? Lime is a beneficial ally for magical as well as physical focus. If you need the magic to focus on one person, place, or thing, or you need the magic of attention, bring lime into your corner. I made a bag for a friend recently, to help them with the MCATs. I placed cotton with a drop of lime oil on it, a pinch of lime zest, their name written over the word "MCAT" on a piece of paper inside it, and 3 clove buds (for luck). They, of course, still worked in the real world, studying and taking practice tests, but having a touchstone to come back to really kept them on their A game.

Loyalty—Having a devoted friend is something everyone deserves and is often more needed than we realize. To draw a loyal friend to you, grab a green candle (earth, fertility, growth), a 10 ml roller bottle, a teaspoon of lime zest or one drop of lime essential oil, and the carrier oil of your choice. Put the zest or drop of lime essential oil into the roller bottle and fill with carrier oil. Cap and roll gently between your palms to mix. Use your new magical pen to draw a downward-pointing arrow on the candle to pull the friend where you are. Internet friends are amazing, but sometimes you need someone close by. Burn the candle on a Sunday for protective energies for the new friendship or a Wednesday for an excellent listener with good communication skills. Either way, that person will be loyal and steadfast.

Overcoming powerlessness—Trauma is a thief. It steals a part of your soul each time. When you are ready to stand up and take those pieces back, reach for lime. Whether it is lime essential oil, or a lime with some salt, this small, brightly-scented fruit has your back. Craft stores have "make your own doll" kits, for dolls that look suspiciously like a poppet because they are. The less crafty among us can learn from Dorothy Morrison and use an eleven-inch fashion doll from the Dollar Store, instead. The cheaper they are, the better they are for bane work. If they're cheaply made and hollow, perfect; this doll is going to be named "Trauma." Rather than hexing a specific person (that can be a separate working), you are going to stop Trauma from stealing your peace, happiness, and power. Zest two limes, and juice them, or grab a bottle of lime essential oil. You'll need cotton balls, permanent markers, and anything that makes you feel powerful. If you have fabulously witchy clothing, put it on. Are you a goddess of the makeup store? Put on your fiercest look. Once you're ready, fill the body cavity with the cotton balls and lime zest, or place lime oil on cotton and stuff inside the doll. Name the doll across the torso, as best you can. Get creative with Trauma. Black out the eyes, so it can't see when you are healthy, to make you doubt yourself. Wrap gauze around the ears so it can't hear you standing up for yourself in the face of adversity. Pour lime juice on it, so it washes away the self-doubt trauma can cause. There is no wrong way with this one. If you want to tear it up or set it on fire, personalizing your trauma and expelling it can be very healing. Yes, it can be healing. It could also be traumatizing. So use it carefully, and, if possible, talk about it with a therapist beforehand. There are free resources available. Most of all, I want you to learn to trust yourself again. How we got here doesn't matter as much as what we choose to do after. No matter what, I believe in you.

Lime Rickey

Tools

- » 4 scotch glasses
- » Pitcher

Ingredients

- » 7 limes (stimulant, strength, focus, healing)
- » 4 oz. simple syrup (love, recovery, uplifting)
- » 12 oz. sparkling water
- » Ice
- » Lime peel for garnish (friendship, love, luck)

Peel a strip of the rind for each of the glasses as a garnish.

Place ice in each glass.

Juice all the limes.

Place simple syrup into a pitcher, add juice, and stir.

Pour the mixed juice into the four glasses (about 3 ounces per glass). Top with sparkling water and garnish.

Toast to your friendship.

Enjoy.

PINE

Botanical Name: Pinus sylvestris

Botanical Family: Pinaceae

World Origin: Australia, Russia, Canada

Part of Plant Used: Needles

Scent Description: Rich, green

Scent Impact: Relieves anxiety

MAGICAL CORRESPONDENCES

Element: Fire

Day: Sunday

Magical Uses: Healing, vitality, purification, friendship

Planet: Sun

Astrological Sign: Libra

Suggested Crystal: Sulfur

Deity/Spirit: Hestia

Warnings: Avoid cheap pine oils, as they are commonly cut with turpentine.

HERBAL LORE AND USES

This laid-back member of the pine family may be found growing out of craggy hilltops, mountain ranges, or cliff faces. This plant knows where other plants fear to tread, and still somehow always wind up there. The oldest living Scots pine is over 210 years old and almost 150 feet (48 meters) tall. This gorgeous specimen lives in Estonia and people will be visiting it for decades to come, as these rough-and-ready dwellers can live up to 300 years old! If you are using the pine essential oil, when you purchase it place a date on the bottle 2 years into the future from date of purchase. Pine oil expires after two years due to oxygenation, and though it won't smell any differently, it can cause contact dermatitis or even sun sensitivity and burns. It is safest to throw away the oil and purchase new. Some students have struggled with this, as waste is so unfortunate. It could theoretically be used in a diffuser for aromatic purposes, or added to homemade candles, but for the very low cost of this oil, it isn't worth getting blisters.

PRACTICAL USES

Friendship in adversity—To cultivate friendships that will withstand difficult times, dilute one drop pine essential oil in a 10 ml roller bottle with jojoba oil. Cap and use to anoint a green (new growth) or brown (stability) candle. Burn on a Wednesday (communication) or Friday (trust with your heart).

Withstanding troubled times—Burn a brown (stability) candle or a pine-scented candle surrounded by fresh pine greenery and branches to increase your ability to stand up to the winds of change. Burn on a Monday (emotional blessing).

Assistance—When assistance is needed, cut a small pine branch from a strong tree (feel free to leave a fertilizer spike or other energetic token to thank the tree). Ask for the help needed. Cast into a swiftly moving body of water, or strip the needles from the branch and cast to the wind.

Purifying the aura—Use fresh pine greenery or a drop of pine essential oil on a reusable cloth. Starting at the head, waft over the body, brushing away etheric dust or cobwebs that lurk on the edges of our energetic body. Brush from top to bottom, on front and back sides.

Awareness of life force—Whether it is the life within all living things or a person's solitary life force, diffuse a drop of pine essential oil in front of you while you breathe deeply, in through the nose and out through the mouth. Keep awareness of your breath for several moments before turning your attention to the life force within you, and without. You may feel texture differences in people's energetic bodies, notice temperature differences, or perceive color.

Balance—To invite balance into your life, anoint a brown (stability) candle with diluted pine essential oil on a Tuesday (victory). Optional: use a pen to write "balance" on the candle before anointing.

Banishing evil and spirits—To banish unwelcome spirits from your home, use a Spirits Be Gone Spray. Steep 4 ounces of fresh pine tips in a pint jar filled with vodka. Allow to macerate for two weeks. Pour 2 ounces into a spray bottle and fill the spray bottle with water. Feel free to add a drop of pine essential oil to the spray if desired. You can fill the pine jar again with 2 ounces of vodka and allow to steep for a full 6 weeks before using again. Spray the home liberally with the spray while you pray in the manner of your tradition, if desired.

Beginnings, renewal—Burn a fire of pine wood or burn pine incense, and write the new beginning desired or the manner of the desired renewal. Anoint the paper with diluted pine essential oil or pine needles. Burn the paper. If fire is difficult in your current situation, use flash paper instead. There will be no heat, smoke, or ashes left behind.

Binding—Binding is a funny word. We want to keep someone from doing something, but unless that person is a loved one (and sometimes even then) what is needed more is banishing. Binding someone binds them to *you*, even if you are attempting to prevent harm. Consider binding carefully. Very young pine branches are flexible. They are flexible enough to make a small circle with a single branch. To bind this person, get a young, thin shoot and some white thread. Tie the end of the thread around the top section of the branch, and bend the end toward the other end of the branch, making a circle. After making a few loops around the end, bind the ends together in a circle. Then take the thread across the circle, loop it around the branch, and come back a few inches away on either side of where you started. Continue back and forth, making an intricate spider web of thread and intent. Picture the binding needed and how it will help the intended target. Once the small spider wreath is complete, set a candle nearby and burn on a Saturday (end bad habits).

Erasing business mistakes—Everyone makes mistakes; we are all human. To give yourself a second chance, write your mistake on a piece (or a few pieces) of flash paper. Be as detailed as you need to be. Anoint the paper with one drop undiluted pine oil and place into a fireproof cauldron or pot. With a lighter or long-necked candle lighter, carefully light the flash paper. There will be a flash of light, but no risk of fire or burns, and no ash to clean up.

Calm, centering—Diffuse a drop of pine essential oil whenever you feel overwhelmed or out of control. Mindful breath will aid you as well.

Courage—Add 3 drops of pine bitters to a 16 ounce glass of water. Raise energy to your hands as described in the beginning of the book. Push the warm, pulsing energy of courage into the water. Drink and feel yourself becoming stronger.

Sober Substitution: Cut a fresh pine twig the length of your palm. Give it a rinse to make sure there are no creatures living on the branch and place it into an 8 ounce glass. Pour boiling water over the leaves ¾ of the way to the top of the glass. Let infuse for 10 minutes before pouring it into a 16 ounce glass. Add a teaspoon of sugar if desired for love and stir to dissolve. Fill the rest of the way with cool water to prevent burning yourself. Drink, envisioning yourself rising to the challenge.

Creativity—To inspire a dormant muse, diffuse pine essential oil in creative spaces 10 minutes to a half hour before entering to begin work. Walking into a clean studio (as clean as any art studio really gets) smelling of pine enlivens the spirit and invigorates the muse. Consider adding a drop of pine oil to a favorite color of paint, or using pine-scented ink to write with as well.

Friendship—To toast a long-term friendship or celebrate a new one, use your dominant hands to anoint one another's palm then touch it to the other person's shoulder or the center of their chest. (Enthusiastic consent!) Or toast using your dominant hand with a shot of homemade (home infused?) pine schnapps (it tastes like Yule!) to project your well wishes to the other person.

Encouraging growth—Growing as a person is hard work. We must always be growing and evolving, or we die. When encountering a difficult situation that can help you grow as a person, place a drop of pine essential oil on a cotton round and keep it in your dominant-handed pocket. Bring out to smell occasionally to calm your mind, relax your body, and remind yourself that things are great. That being said, if you feel like something is *wrong*, and not just low-grade anxiety, examine it. We know anxiety lies to us, but sometimes there is something going on. Be as safe as you can out there.

Inner guidance—When it is time to learn to listen to your inner voice, and not the anxiety that mimics your inner voice, it's time to sit with our friend, pine. Diffuse pine oil during meditation, burn pine incense, or place a drop of pine essential oil in water on your oil burner. The most important part is opening up a dialogue with yourself, both the anxious parts and the self-aware parts. The more often you practice this, the more readily you can piece together whether or not it is a real voice or anxiety talking.

Harmony of a space—To encouraging harmony in a space, diffuse a drop of pine essential oil in a room that feels unbalanced. If you don't have a diffuser on hand, you can add 5 drops of pine oil to a cup of salt, stir, and set it out in the space to evaporate over time. You can also put a splash of rubbing alcohol or witch hazel in the bottom of a spray bottle, add a few drops of pine oil, and swirl to mix. Then just top off the bottle with a bit of water, and mist the space as much as you'd like.

Harmony in relationships—Talk out issues over a pine fire, pine schnapps, or while burning pine incense. Apologizing if you are at fault is great, but don't be bullied into apologizing if you didn't do anything wrong.

Hex breaking—Anoint a black candle (banishing) with "hex breaking" inscribed on it. Anoint it with diluted pine oil and burn on a Saturday (endings).

Justice—Pine works for justice because it seeks balance and restores calm. Unjust situations get upsetting really quickly! Anoint a blue candle with "justice" written on it for justly dismissing a lawsuit before it can get to court. Burn it on a Saturday (endings). If it needs to go to court to get justice, anoint a yellow candle (thought) with patchouli oil for a Just Judge, and a purple candle (divine justice). Burn them on a Sunday.

Knowledge, learning—To open yourself to the knowledge of the universe, anoint a black candle (limitlessness of space) with pine oil. Write "knowledge" on it and burn it on a Wednesday (communication).

Increasing libido—Dilute 1 drop of pine oil in a 10 ml roller bottle; anoint a red candle with an up arrow and the word "sex" or "libido." Optional: include a name for specificity.

Pine Sugar

Tools

- » Rolling pin
- » Pint jar

Ingredients

- » 16 oz. raw sugar (love, fertility)
- » 4 oz. freshly harvested pine needles (friendship in adversity, centering, courage, growth)

Lay the fresh pine needles out on the counter. Gently roll over them with a rolling pin two or three times to release the scent without releasing chlorophyll. Layer in a pint jar, alternating pine needles and sugar until the jar is filled. Cap and let aroma develop over 2–3 weeks. Obviously the longer it sits, the more developed the fragrance and flavor. Add to teas, coffee, baked goods, and more. Use anywhere the magic of pine is desired.

Pine Bitters

Tools

- » Quart glass jar with lid
- » Strainer
- » 12 oz. bottle

Ingredients

- » 8 oz. vodka (love, protection)

- » 4 oz. freshly harvested pine needles (balance, beginnings, peace, prosperity, protection, purification)
- » 2 oz. simple syrup
- » 1 very small piece angelica root (divine protection, dispelling negativity, psychic protection, binding evil)

Fill the jar with as much pine as you can. Include the wood, too; it gives a more developed flavor and a lovely reddish color to the drink. Angelica is very earthy, so if you like a bitter, earthy flavor, feel free to use a slightly larger piece.

Place the angelica on top of the pine needles and cover with vodka. Let macerate for 4–6 weeks. Strain out the herbal material and transfer to the larger bottle.

Add the simple syrup. Cap, shake, and store in the refrigerator.

Pine Schnapps

Tools

- » Rolling pin
- » Quart glass jar with lid
- » Strainer
- » 16 oz. bottle

Ingredients

- » 8 oz. vodka (love, protection)
- » 4 oz. freshly harvested pine needles (balance, beginnings, peace, prosperity, protection, purification)
- » 4 oz. simple syrup

Lay the fresh pine needles out on the counter. Gently roll over them with a rolling pin two or three times to release the scent without releasing chlorophyll.

Fill the jar with as much pine as you can. Include the wood, too; it gives a more developed flavor and a lovely reddish color to the drink.

Cover the pine needles with vodka. Let macerate for 4–6 weeks. Strain out the herbal material and transfer the liquid to the larger bottle.

Add simple syrup. Cap, shake, and store in the refrigerator.

STRAWBERRY

Botanical Name: Fragaria virginiana, F. × ananassa, others

Botanical Family: Rosaceae

World Origin: Various

Part of Plant Used: Fruit

Scent Description: Sweet, pink, fruity

Scent Impact: N/A

MAGICAL CORRESPONDENCES

Element: Water

Day: Friday

Magical Uses: Attraction, beauty, friendship, respect, visions

Planet: Venus

Astrological Sign: Taurus

Suggested Crystal: Pietersite (green or red/brown)

Deity/Spirit: Freya, Isis

Warnings: Generally regarded as safe.

HERBAL LORE AND USES

The common garden strawberry that is enjoyed throughout North America is known as the Virginia strawberry. The more enormous variety grown for its size, aroma, and appearance is a hybrid offspring of the Virginia species, bred in France. There are over twenty varieties of *Fragaria,* and their offspring number collectively in the thousands.

When hulled and sliced, these delicate and easily bruised fruit (technically they are not a true berry) resemble a lovely, red heart. That's no coincidence, as these delectable, bite-sized members of the rose family are associated with Venus (as are all stone fruits).

PRACTICAL USES

Attraction—Signal your intention to a potential romantic interest by sharing this juicy berry with them. Muddle strawberries with lime to attract a love interest who is happy, loyal, and respects you. If you're looking for a sexy roll in the hay, chop apples and strawberries and add a dash of cinnamon before topping with sparkling apple cider in a champagne flute.

Beauty—Eating these berries when in season is a great way to provide omega-3 and -6 and vitamin C. Vitamin C takes the redness out of skin and has a mild acid content. Because of that, and due to their other natural acids, strawberries make a lovely face mask with oatmeal for balancing the oil/dry factors in skin's makeup. The omega fatty acids are great for hair, nails, and more. Eating strawberries is associated with beauty, for good reason. Offer a handful of berries to Venus, Aphrodite, Freya, or Isis, and keep a handful for yourself.

Mental flexibility—The aforementioned omega fatty acids are also great for keeping your brain in shape. These oils found in large quantities in fish oils are a supplement commonly suggested for attention span, mental acuity, and more. Leave a bowl of strawberries out for Athena, Minerva, or The Morrigan if you need quick thinking to save the day. Strategy is Their middle name.

Fortune—This isn't simple money we are talking about. For everyday prosperity there are lots of hardworking herbs, fruits, woods, and flowers to turn to. For the true blessings of (good) fortune, leave a bowl of ripe, beautiful strawberries for Fortuna (Tyche in Greece) and ask that she look well upon you. This daughter of Jupiter (Zeus in Greece) will be especially happy if you do it on her father's day, Thursday.

Friendship—To attract a new friend, sit down with a small bowl of strawberries and a candle (best on a Friday), and call out to Philotes, the Greek goddess of social intercourse, friendship, and affection. As the daughter of Nyx (the goddess of night), she is intimately aware of how loving friendships do in dark times. Light a candle in her honor, and gift her half your berries. With the remaining berries, name a trait your ideal friend will have. For bonus points, try finding an image of her for her worship, even if it is printed from an image search. The strawberries are a lovely offering as she is one of the few gods who rebuked animal sacrifices in Ancient Greece.

Harmony—Peacekeeping, whether for romantic, platonic, or familial relationships, is a necessary skill. To inspire peace among loved ones, wash and bless a bowl of strawberries, then serve them as a treat for everyone. With the hull (or the top leaves) serve with homemade whipped cream; without the hull, consider dusting them with sugar and serving over pound cake for the fullness of love and emotional vulnerability.

Joy—Make a simple syrup by boiling one cup water, adding one cup sugar, and whisking until clear. Next, muddle 5 (the number associated with Venus) strawberries and add them to the syrup. Flavor seltzer (creativity, spontaneity) with it for a joyous pick-me-up. (For more information on syrups, check out Chapter 8.)

Relaxation—Get your spa vibes at home or in the ritual circle. Strawberries are equated with the magic of relaxation and have been for countless years. Slice a pint of fresh, freshly washed strawberries, and place them into a pitcher of cold water. Enjoy with friends, or with your best friend, yourself. Learning to like who we are is hard work, but worthwhile.

Sensuality and romantic relationships—Venus's influence strikes again. The strawberries are seen as the union of opposites, fruit with visible seeds, as well as the womb-shaped void inside the fruit itself. To improve heterosexual relationships, try having you and your partner feed each other strawberries blessed and prepared with whipped cream, chocolate sauce, or powdered sugar. For masculine-only partnerships, add banana, not for the obvious reasons, but because the original Mars fruit, bananas, were more seed than they were fruit. For feminine partnerships, add some diced apple to the mix.

Spirit—To nurture our own spirit, as many of us are usually taking care of others, prepare a tea of the dried strawberry hulls, or by adding warm water and honey to muddled strawberry.

Visions—Mental flexibility also extends to the psychic as well as the day-to-day. To encourage visions, intuitions, and more, meditation is the answer. Psychic visions and insights are the results of learning your own intuitive language. For a love triangle, you may see a triangle in your mind's eye, or you may see a traffic circle. To expand your mind, find the most perfect strawberry in the bunch, and hold it in your hands for a few moments. Examine all the sides, where the leaves attach to the berry, the depth of the seeds in the flesh, and every other detail. Smell the berry; memorize the scent of it. Close your eyes and envision the fruit in your mind. Every exacting detail is there for you. When you have recreated the scent, color, texture, and more, eat the berry. Allow the juice to fill your mouth with taste and aroma. Try this for a few days in a row until you can build your own berry from scratch. Then try other fruits and vegetables. We are building your language just the way we did when teaching babies to speak. You are associating language with words and ideas.

Aiding in childbirth—Carry a small pouch with dried strawberries in it, for the last few weeks of pregnancy. If you're traveling with your go bag, put the strawberries in there too as a talisman for a smooth delivery.

RECIPES

Sensual Strawberry Lavender Lemonade

Tools

- » Pitcher

Ingredients

- » 2 cups lavender syrup—see Chapter 8 (attraction, love, harmony, friendship)
- » 1½ cups water
- » 7 lemons—about a cup lemon juice (ability, abundance, fidelity)
- » 1 cup strawberry puree (balance, harmony, peace, centering)

Strawberry Puree

Tools

- » Food processor

Ingredients

- » ½ pint of strawberries
- » ¼ cup of sugar

Place the strawberries and sugar into the food processor bowl and pulse.

Note: frozen berries are likely dyed with FD&C Red 40 or some other coloring agent, since the freezing process removes color.

Place the strawberry puree in a pitcher, add lavender syrup, and stir.

Pour the lemon juice into the mixture and stir again.

Add water and stir until well blended.

Garnish with strawberries and a pinch of lavender.

Enjoy with someone you fancy.

VANILLA

Scientific name: Vanilla planifolia

Botanical Family: Orchidaceae

World Origin: Mexico, Central America

Part of Plant Used: Fruit

Scent Description: Soft, creamy, woody, paperlike

Scent Factor: Strong

Evaporation: Base note

Scent Impact: Calming, comforting, release of tension in the body

MAGICAL CORRESPONDENCES

Application: Inhalation, diffusion

Element: Water

Day: Friday

Magical Uses: Calm, clarity, love, thought

Planet: Venus

Astrological Sign: Scorpio

Suggested Crystal: Amber

Deity/Spirit: Maeve

Warnings: Fruit is generally regarded as safe.

HERBAL LORE AND USES

This delicately scented seed pod is not a bean at all. It contains millions of tiny seeds that give vanilla syrup its signature flavor. These plants are slow growing and do not produce their fruit until they reach ten feet tall (three or more meters). Due to its humidity needs, this orchid is largely propagated inside greenhouses and, in warmer climates, open-air pavilions with armatures made of bamboo. Because of the special treatment and handling it requires, the vanilla orchid is pollinated by hand by trained caregivers. Special care must be taken as each flower produces only one pod, and it must mature on the vine for five months before being delicately harvested and fermented. Special clothing is required for the handling of this lovely yellow flowering plant, as the sap coming in contact with the skin results in contact dermatitis. Washing with soap and water as soon as exposure is noticed is the key to reducing irritation from the calcium oxalate crystals found in the orchid's sap.

Vanilla planifolia contains many chemical compounds, but the most prevalent are 4-hydroxybenzaldehyde, vanillin, 4-hydroxybenzoic acid, and vanillic acid. Vanillin is the same chemical compound that is produced in cellulose during the decomposition process. So, when someone tells you he loves the smell of old books, he is praising true vanilla for its aroma. When purchasing the essential oil, look for the words "vanilla CO_2" and 12 percent vanillin to ensure you are getting the highest quality you can fit into your budget.

PRACTICAL USES

Calming aggression, comfort—Place a vanilla bean in your sugar bowl to add a light vanilla flavor and fragrance to the sweetener. Each time the sugar is used, it imparts loving calm to any who enjoy it.

Dreams—Put a vanilla pod inside a blue cloth bag and place it inside your pillowcase for a peaceful dream state.

Balance—Diffuse a drop of vanilla essential oil in a space that is feeling out of sorts, to restore balance to the home.

Attraction—To signal to the universe that you're ready for a new loving relationship, dilute 3 drops of vanilla essential oil into a 10 ml roller bottle filled with carrier oil. Use it to draw a heart symbol onto a red candle and burn it on a Friday.

Mental powers, focus, clarity—To regain your center and see through the fog of illness, confusion, or other issues, make a tin of black tea, in which vanilla pods are cut into small chips or pieces. Mix thoroughly and place in an air- and light-tight container. Add 2 teaspoons of tea to 8 ounces of hot water. Steep for 5 minutes before removing the tea leaves and sweetening if desired. Breathe in through the nose and out through the mouth while visualizing the fog lifting, and drink.

Restorative—After feeling sick, run-down, or lethargic, diffuse 1 drop of vanilla essential oil in your space for 10 minutes while practicing mindful breath. Repeat three times a day if needed until your old self has returned.

Passion—Give your romantic partner a small pouch made of red fabric containing a small piece of vanilla pod and a cotton ball that has 1 drop of vanilla essential oil on it. If you can craft the bag on a Friday, all the better. Their passion will return.

Relaxing—When you've forgotten how to relax and it's time to remember for your sake, blend a cup of honeybush tea leaves with two chopped vanilla bean pods. Brew 1½ teaspoons of tea for 8 ounces of hot water. Steep 5 minutes. Store the remaining tea in an airtight container.

Peace—Anoint a pale blue candle with diluted vanilla essential oil and see peace coming into your life. For best results, drink a cup of chamomile tea sweetened with vanilla sugar while meditating on what peace looks like.

Love, desire—Vanilla pods that have been used for tincturing or flavoring can be dried and added to incense for love and a creamy, woody scent.

Energy—You wouldn't think such a calming, comforting smell would be associated with energy, but this plant holds many surprises. The restorative effects of this fruit are energizing because they remind us what life was like before we were so tired. Diffuse vanilla during mornings when you didn't get quite enough sleep, but still need to be on your A game.

Fortune—Looking to turn away a streak of bad luck? Dilute 3 drops of vanilla essential oil into a 10 ml roller bottle filled with carrier. (Jojoba or fractionated coconut are the best for long shelf life.) Anoint pulse points, wrists, behind each ear, and behind the knees. Then anoint a yellow or gold candle with the vanilla oil on a Sunday, and burn until finished.

Gambling luck—Take a 10 ml roller bottle with vanilla essential oil and carrier oil, and anoint each palm in a clockwise circle in the center of the palm to draw gambling luck and money to your palms.

Harmony—To restore harmony in the home after an argument or upheaval, diffuse vanilla essential oil.

Happiness—On an orange or yellow candle, inscribe a happy, smiling face. Anoint the candle with diluted vanilla essential oil and burn on a Sunday.

Divine inspiration—Do you have a project sitting around collecting dust while you wait for inspiration? Anoint a purple candle with diluted vanilla essential oil and burn on a Wednesday or during the full moon.

Marriage—To signal to a partner that you are ready for marriage, serve iced vanilla vodka or vanilla tea (or make it a tea cocktail!) to signal that you're in a stable and loving place with room for passion and romance.

Meditation—Light incense charcoal and burn vanilla pods as you concentrate on your mindful breath. Visualizing your intended outcome during this time is also beneficial.

RECIPES

Guardian of the Peace Cordial

Tools

» Bottle

Ingredients

» 3 cups 100 proof vodka (protection)

» ½ cup simple syrup (mood elevating)

» 2 vanilla pods (calm, peace, restorative)

Place a splash of vodka into the bottle where the cordial will macerate.

Carefully cut each pod lengthwise and scrape out the seeds.

Add the vanilla seeds into the bottle with pods.

Pour the rest of the vodka into the bottle. Place the lid on the bottle and store in a cool, dark place.

Let sit for 4 weeks, shaking occasionally.

After 4 weeks, add ½ cup simple syrup, cap the bottle, and shake.

Serve with calm and loving friends.

More Fun in the Kitchen

When creating your own potions for the well-being of your family, consider these traditional remedies. You can make them before they are needed so you'll have them on hand when the situation arises.

FIRE CIDER

This folk remedy is touted as being as old as the stars, but has no real mention prior to the 1970s, and most people had never heard of it until recently. This blend of spicy vegetables and roots galore is steeped in apple cider vinegar for a few weeks to a month, until it is ready to drink! Onion, horseradish, garlic, hot peppers, and ginger? I'll admit it, the first time someone mentioned it to me I was pretty skeptical. Then late winter arrives and everyone is sick and you're desperate so you'll try *anything*. I was pleasantly surprised. It has a bit of a cinnamon bite to it, and it is vinegar-based, so I thought it would be flavored like rank pickles. It was delightful. Entire books are devoted to this folk remedy for colds, the flu, and other winter crud. What I'm providing here is intended to just whet your appetite. You can sip a few teaspoons of this three times a day when you feel a cold coming on. Some put a teaspoon in juice every morning to ward off illness. You can also add it to soups and chilis and make sure the whole family is inoculated. You can make it into a salad dressing for a little heat. Plus, once the veggies are scooped out, they taste amazing in a stir fry.

CONTROVERSY OVER THE NAME "FIRE CIDER"

In 2014 an herbal folk remedies company, Shire City Herbals, started making and marketing its own version of the popular folk remedy. Normally this wouldn't be an issue as folk remedies are considered generic and the names available for general use. The problem arose when Shire City started issuing cease and desist letters to small farms and women-owned businesses who were also selling their own fire ciders. Because this is not a strict recipe, and more "feel it out until it looks right," folk herbalists all over were shocked that a recipe that has been in popular use since the 1970s and was published in other books in the mid 1990s could be claimed in trademark. The small, independent businesses involved in the suit fought back, eventually winning their case in late 2019, establishing folk remedy solidarity for years to come.

Why is this important? Folk herbalism medicines are available to everyone, without the cost of heavy medical bills and doctor visits. These remedies are free information that is shared the world over, though the specific recipe will differ from person to person. The same goes for another folk herbalism cure, known as Four Thieves Vinegar. During the Black Plague, the story goes that four men were robbing the graves of plague victims, and when they were caught by the townspeople whose loved ones were being robbed, the captors offered the thieves their lives in exchange for the recipe. Each thief put a botanical in the vinegar, and they drank it before going out grave robbing. The recipe varies from person to person and story to story. The problem comes in when popular essential oil companies trademark the name of a folk herbal treatment and use it to sell their own version, and attack companies who had been making this vinegar for decades before the companies were founded. When we take the cures out of the hands of the people, we are putting a price tag on the health and well-being of fragile communities.

Fire Cider

Tools

» Quart jar with lid

Ingredients

» 2–3 cups apple cider vinegar—with the Mother for probiotic benefit

» 1 orange, sliced (strength, prosperity, stimulating, relaxing)

» 1 lemon, sliced (calming, clarity, energy, banishing fatigue)

» ½ cup horseradish, diced—grab a jar if you can't find fresh (protection, vitality)

» ½ cup parsley, chopped (banishing negativity)

» ½cup garlic (protection, health, vitality)

» ½ cup diced onion (protection, banishing negativity)

» ¼ cup raw honey or more to taste (sweetness, fulfillment)

» ¼ cup diced ginger (protection, luck, healing)

» 1 habanero, split in half and deseeded (power, protection, luck)

» 2 tbsp. rosemary (hex breaking, healing, protection)

» 2 tbsp. thyme (awareness, courage, purification)

» 1 tsp. black peppercorns (banishing, protection, purification)

Chop all ingredients, place into a clean quart jar, and fill with apple cider vinegar. It needs to sit in a dark, cool cabinet for a few weeks until it is ready. I usually say 4–5 weeks, but I usually remember it's in the cabinet about 8 weeks later. Then you can strain out the material, add honey until you don't hate sipping it, and enjoy!

KOMBUCHA

This probiotic-rich drink is your new biological best friend. The star of the kombucha story is the *SCOBY*. SCOBY is the acronym for Symbiotic Culture Of Bacteria and Yeast, meaning that this drink is alive! We will be growing a living colony of beneficial bacteria and yeast. As mammals we have a complex system of bacteria and yeasts that are naturally occurring in our bodies all the time. (I won't go into specifics for the body-horror folks, but it is fascinating reading.)

For anyone sensitive to alcohol, the by-product of the tea fermenting is alcohol, at 0.5–1 percent. This isn't enough for the drink to be considered an alcoholic beverage, but those with a sensitivity to alcohol should be aware.

For a gallon of kombucha you will need:

- » 2 cups of kombucha
- » 1 gallon of water
- » 8 tea bags
- » 1 cup of sugar
- » 1 SCOBY (handle gently; it's a living thing, and rough handling can kill it)

Kombucha SCOBY

So you won't need to beg for a SCOBY from a friend, we're going to make our own.

Tools

- » Glass mixing bowl
- » Large widemouthed jar
- » Several tea towels or other layered, closely woven fabric to cover mouth of jar

Ingredients

» 1 cup of your favorite, unflavored, nonpasteurized kombucha

» 2 cups water

» ½ cup granulated sugar (avoid alternative sugars due to potential contamination and other issues)

» 4 unflavored black tea bags of your choice (you can use green tea for the kombucha, but for growing a SCOBY, use the black tea)

Wash any bottles, jars, spoons, and the like. If possible, use the *hot* cycle on the dishwasher to sterilize them before use.

Boil 2 cups of water, and pour it into a glass bowl. Add sugar and stir to dissolve. Add 4 unflavored black tea bags of your choice. Allow to steep for 10 minutes before removing them. Add 5 cups of cool water to bring down the temperature.

Add the tea to a large, widemouthed jar. Next add the kombucha and give it a gentle stir. If you see wispy things floating in your store-bought kombucha, make sure to include them. That's what will grow into your SCOBY.

Cover the mouth of the jar with the several layers of fabric. While cheesecloth might seem like the thing, it can still allow fruit flies and other organisms inside the jar. You want the air to move freely, without any outside nasties getting in. The nature of the SCOBY is to protect the kombucha from bad bacteria or yeasts, the cloth helps during the vulnerable stage when the SCOBY is developing. Make sure that the room where you'll be brewing your tea is around 70°. The warmer your room is, the faster the SCOBY will develop. Leave it in an undisturbed place for 1–4 weeks. The longer it sits there, the more established it will be. Make sure to thoroughly wash your hands before touching the SCOBY so as not to transfer harmful bacteria to it. Make sure it is out of sunlight, in an area with a stable temperature, and not near any heating or cooling vents.

You will notice bubbles forming on the surface of the tea after a few days to a week. The fermentation has started. Those bubbles will join together to take over the world! No, wrong movie. They'll start forming a thick layer that will become the fully developed SCOBY. You'll want that to be at least ¼ inch thick to start making your own kombucha. The first generation or two will look bumpy and bubbly, but as it matures, those developing layers will smooth out.

Once it is thick enough to remove, it'll be ready to make kombucha. The liquid the SCOBY was made from will be too vinegary to drink but will work as a starter for the kombucha, and the rest can be used to clean stove tops and counters.

It should smell tart and vinegary.

If you see black or green spots or if it smells cheesy, bad, or rancid, it's been contaminated. Start over. If you aren't sure, leave it alone. Either it's okay, or the smell will get worse. In that case, you can get rid of it.

• • •

Now that you have your SCOBY ready, we can get back to brewing the kombucha.

Boil 4 cups of water. Add sugar and stir until dissolved. Pour into the large fermenting jug.

Add the tea bags and allow them to steep 15 minutes.

Add 2½ quarts of water to the jug and remove the tea bags.

Stir in kombucha. (This makes the tea acidic enough to inhibit bad bacteria and yeast from forming.)

Gently transfer in a SCOBY. If you have more than one (they peel apart in layers) you can produce multiple batches simultaneously. Only one SCOBY per jar is needed. Cover the mouth of the jar with a tea towel and a rubber band to hold it in place.

Ferment 7–10 days; the shorter the time the less vinegary it will taste. The flavor will develop the longer it is in contact with the SCOBY/ Mother. Just give a little sip each day after 7 days and keep it fermenting until it reaches the sweetness/tartness balance that tastes right to you.

Then it is ready to transfer to the secondary bottles. Remember to set aside 2 cups of kombucha for the next batch you're going to make.

If you want to infuse your brew with fruits for extra flavor and magic, see Chapter 8. Just put fruit, juice, or other flavorings in a separate jar without Mother to infuse for 2 days before bottling. When bottling, leave 2 inches of headspace. Leave on a counter out of direct sunlight for 1–3 days to develop carbonation. Refrigerate after carbonated, and drink within a lunar cycle.

For more on this subject, with glorious photos, check out *True Brews: How to Craft Fermented Cider, Beer, Wine, Sake, Soda, Mead, and Kombucha at Home* by Emma Christensen.

GINGER BUG

If you like the idea of kombucha but the flavor just isn't there for you, the Ginger Bug might be just where you want to be. Ginger Bug is a wild fermented beverage with probiotic benefits just like its tea-based counterpart. It makes a naturally carbonated soda where you control what goes into it and, more importantly, what doesn't go into it.

Ginger magic is that of energizing and stimulating, of power and passion. This soda can be empowered to give you strength, prosperity, courage, and luck. (There's an entire section on the awesomeness that is ginger in magic in *Blackthorn's Botanical Magic* if you want to do more with this spicy root.)

The ingredients are simple—water, ginger, sugar—but the uses are so much more. They support metabolic health and the immune system, and benefit digestion.

Buy organic ginger if you can. It hasn't been irradiated and will more readily have surface yeast from the air to ferment with.

Don't peel; that's where the natural yeast will live.

Dice ginger. It's easier to scoop it out later and it works better.

Sugar is great. It can be raw or granulated—just don't try calorie-free sweeteners; they don't work.

Don't use chlorinated tap water; it'll kill the wild yeast we need to make the carbonation. Filter the chlorine out or buy bottled.

Unlike the kombucha, Ginger Bug needs a tight-fitting lid that can stand up to the pressures of carbonation, such as Fido jars for canning or reusable beer bottles from a brewing supply store. Not all bail-top bottles are suitable for carbonation. Use caution.

Tools

» Saucepan

» Jar or bottle suitable for carbonation

Ingredients

» 2 tsp. sugar

» 1 oz. fresh ginger, diced

» 2 cups of water

Think of the magic of ginger and what you want the soda to grow (this will be growing a bacteria colony like yogurt), whether it be health, money, passion, or courage. Put that intention into each step of the process. Pour the water into the saucepan. Charge the ginger, envisioning the outcome while the water heats. Put the sugar into the saucepan and stir until it dissolves. Take the diced ginger and place it into the jar with kind words about your intended magical outcome. Let the sugar water cool then pour it over the ginger. Close the lid and allow it to sit at room temperature for a day.

After the first day, open the lid and feed the bug a teaspoon of sugar and another ½ ounce of ginger. Repeat your intention while you stir. Place the lid back on the jar. Do this every day for 5 days. After the third day (and as late as the fifth day, if it is cold) you should start to see bubbles start to form signaling the fermentation is steadily working.

Spice up your life! Pour ½ cup of the ginger bug into 7½ cups of fruit juice or sweetened tea. Try combinations to further your magical intent: ginger apple cider for passionate lovers; ginger orange juice for an inspirational friend, ginger-rose black tea for a courageous love who will protect your heart.

INFUSED VINEGARS

This is the easiest thing to do in the kitchen to have people thinking you're a gourmet genius. These can be made into marinades, salad dressings, and so much more. You'll need:

- » Bail-topped bottles or jars
- » Apple cider vinegar
- » Herbs

Chickweed

This spring I made a delightful herbal vinegar with the first cover crop of the season: chickweed! It contains lots of vitamin C, calcium, and magnesium. Some recipes call for pureeing the chickweed, but it isn't necessary. You'll need:

Tools

- » Colander
- » Bail-topped jar

Ingredients

- » ½ cup apple cider vinegar—with Mother; remember the probiotic benefits of unpasteurized apple cider vinegar
- » 2 handfuls of chickweed, fresh from the garden

It's okay if you don't plant it; it's the first weed to pop up before the gardens get tilled and planted. It is a pale green plant with tiny, white, star-shaped flowers. Rinse the bugs and dirt off by tossing it in a colander and spraying with water. Give it a shake to remove the water and place it into a bail-topped jar. Pour the vinegar over the plant material to the top.

Let sit for 4 weeks, shaking every so often. The magic of chickweed is joy, prosperity, and the blessings of nature.

Lemon Balm

I made this in the summer with a bumper crop of lemon balm. It's a member of the mint family so it goes *everywhere*. I cut it back, and it springs up somewhere else. (Don't take this wrong; I plant it everywhere.) This is an easy and flavorful way to use this sedative plant that showcases its bright and sweet flavor. Lemon balm magic is that of success, compassion, and prosperity, and is blessed by the goddess Diana. It is uplifting; it soothes emotional wounds and instills love. You'll need:

Tools

» 10 oz. bail-topped bottle

Ingredients

» ½ oz. dried lemon balm

» Enough apple cider vinegar to fill bottle

Pour the dried lemon balm into the bottle. Fill with apple cider vinegar and allow to sit for 6 weeks to infuse. Mix with olive oil for a delicious salad dressing. (See Chapter 6 for more vinegar ideas.)

Once you have a vinegar you love, combine 4 parts oil to 1 part vinegar to create a delightful salad dressing that can't be beaten. Don't forget to add salt and pepper to taste.

Grapefruit and Thyme

This bright and zesty vinegar is ready in a day or two and keeps well on the shelf.

Tools

- » 1 small bowl
- » Strainer

Ingredients

- » 1 perfect grapefruit
- » 3 cups apple cider vinegar
- » 1 tsp. dried thyme or 1 tbsp. fresh thyme

Slice the grapefruit and place into a small bowl. Pour the apple cider vinegar over the sliced grapefruit and add one teaspoon dried thyme or a tablespoon of fresh thyme. Give the brew a quick stir, cover it with a tea towel if you wish, and leave it on the counter for 2 days for the best flavor. Strain out the fruit and herbs, label, and bottle.

Botanical Brews
in the Bar

When creating potions and brews of the *spirited* variety, your only limit is your imagination—smoked cocktails for purification, tea-based cocktails for the connoisseur, and infused alcohols for the do-it-yourself enthusiasts among us. In this chapter, we will be looking at creating our own infused liquors and bitters, and making use of the imagination inside us all.

INFUSED LIQUORS

One of the easiest ways to power your potion and boost your brew is to add botanicals to your spirits for extra flavor, personality, and kick. Your plain-Jane martini becomes a Werewolves of London martini, or a vanilla- and lavender-infused daydream.

How do we do this? It's deceptively easy and more complicated than it sounds. "Just throw stuff in there," is the short answer, but it can lead to some interesting experiments. Garden sage-infused vodka seemed like a neat idea for a smoky cocktail but ended up falling flat. The best part of the experiments is they can wind up making fabulous magical components. That sage vodka made an excellent base for a cleansing spray with essential oils for when I don't have the energy for smoke cleansing my entire house. It's a great spot clean.

Sage-Infused Vodka and Room-Cleansing Spray

Tools

» 1 pint jar with lid

Ingredients

» Vodka (protection, luck, money)

» Fresh garden sage (cleansing, consecration, divination, protection)

» Optional: fresh rosemary (smarts, antianxiety, balance, concentration)

Fill the jar with broad-leaved culinary sage, then smush more in there after it looks full—this is when you'll add the fresh rosemary, if you like. Add the vodka and let it sit for 8 weeks before giving it a taste test. It should be very earthy, with some loam flavors as well.

For the room-cleansing spray mentioned above you'll need a spray bottle, Sage Infused Vodka, rosemary essential oil, and water. Pour $^1/_8$ of the spray bottle's volume of sage vodka (about 1½ cups) and 5 drops of rosemary essential oil into the spray bottle. Fill the bottle the rest of the way with water, and give it a shake. Spray in areas that need uplifting and energetic cleansing.

Limoncello

I have made these from various citrus fruits as Yule gifts for years. I use the slightly more labor-intensive version for a slightly better outcome, but everyone swears the quick method is still bright and sunny.

Super Quick Limoncello

Tools

- » Bowl
- » Sterilized bottles

Ingredients

- » 2 lemons, sliced ¼"–½" thick (abundance, action, balance, friendship, purification, fidelity)
- » 8 oz. vodka (protection)
- » 8 oz. simple syrup—see Chapter 8 for more information (love, lust, protection)

Pour vodka into a bowl.

Place lemon slices into vodka.

Leave overnight. Feel free to cover with a tea towel to protect from bugs, dust, or pet hair.

Strain into bottle.

Add simple syrup.

Stir and enjoy.

Remember, this can work with any citrus; lemon is merely traditional.

Two-Day Limoncello

Tools

- » Zester
- » Bowl
- » Sterilized bottles

Ingredients

- » 3 lemons (calming, clarity, divination, focus, happiness)
- » 8 oz. vodka (protection)
- » 8 oz. simple syrup (love, lust, protection)

Slicing the lemons will allow the juice and the pith to add to the flavor of your final product. Instead, zest your fruit. You can make lemonade with it when you're done zesting to reduce waste. (Don't wait longer than that. The zest keeps the fruit juicy, and, once it is zested off, the fruit dries rapidly and loses flavor.)

Pour vodka into a bowl.

Zest as much of the lemon peel as possible while visualizing your goal.

Place zest into vodka.

Leave for 2 days, stirring once a day. Again, cover if desired

Strain into bottle.

Add simple syrup.

Stir and enjoy.

This recipe is the way my Italian great-aunt taught me to make it. When I made this version for a Yule party, it was lauded as better than a Parisian couple who used to wander the streets selling booze in underground cafes. It was the most legitimate I have felt about the joys of "magical boozery," so it's the one I recommend if you aren't on a timeline. The most popular version of this came about the year I got a case of tangerines from a friend's son selling fruit for a school club. It tasted like sunshine, and everyone loved it. The oleosaccharum from Chapter 8 would be a lovely addition to our "-cello" recipes. Feel free to play around with the amounts as this would be the longest recipe of the three.

Cranberry-Infused Triple Sec

Tools

» 1 pint jar

» Muddler

Ingredients

» ½ cup cranberries (healing, inspiration, protection, release of tension)

» A sprinkle of raw sugar

» Triple sec

Muddle ½ cup of cranberries in a pint jar with a sprinkle of raw sugar to help break down the berries. Fill the jar with triple sec, cap, and wait 6 weeks.

Please see Witch's Poinsettia Punch, page 172.

Pine-Infused Vodka

Tools

» 1 pint jar

Ingredients

» 1 dense handful of white pine needles and twigs (fertility, money, protection)

» 8-ish oz. vodka (protection)

When taking down the Yule tree, my family cuts some of the tender young ends off the tree (we don't use fake snow, obviously) until we have a dense handful of greenery and twigs. We then cram them into a pint jar. Get as much greenery in there as possible. Fill the jar with vodka. (Don't use grain alcohol; too much alcohol causes cell damage.) Let sit 3-4 weeks, shaking occasionally.

Once the clear vodka becomes a dark red/brown, it is time to strain out the plant material. The vodka can then be stored in another similar jar or bottle. When the post-holiday blues start to rear their ugly heads, grab a little Yule cheer.

Please see Post-Holiday Slump Spritz, page 173.

Earl Grey Tea-Infused Gin

Tools

 » Pint jar

Ingredients

 » 8 ounces of dry gin

 » 1 tbsp. of your favorite Earl Grey tea

Put the tea and dry gin into the pint jar. Let sit 6–8 weeks in a cool, dark cabinet before straining and bottling. Add one ounce at a time to gin martinis.

Please see Werewolves of London Martini Tea Cocktail, page 173.

Vanilla and Cinnamon-Infused Whiskey

Tools

 » 1 pint jar

Ingredients

- » 9 oz. whiskey (abundance, advice, wealth, growth)
- » 7 oz. simple syrup (love, banishing depression, preservation, recovery)
- » 3 vanilla beans (or 2 tsp. vanilla bean paste) (calm, passion, relaxing)
- » 3 cinnamon sticks (creativity, luck, enthusiasm, protection, uplifting)

Place cinnamon sticks into the jar.

Add simple syrup to the jar.

Cut vanilla bean in half lengthwise, scrape out the seeds, and add to the potion.

Fill the jar the rest of the way with whiskey.

Cap and place on a dark shelf for 24 hours.

After 24 hours, remove the cinnamon sticks.

Optional: Place the sticks into an 8 oz. glass jar and fill most of the way with sugar. Place a lid on the jar. Shake once a day for the first week. It will be ready after a month. Cinnamon-flavored sugar is excellent in coffee, tea, and pancakes.

Continue to infuse the vanilla beans for another week before use.

Vanilla bean doesn't need to be removed.

Please see Love Lies Bleeding Cocktail, page 174.

Homemade Vanilla Extract

Tools

- » 12 oz. bail-topped bottle

Ingredients

- » 11 oz. dark rum or whiskey—100 proof minimum (love, lust, recovery, preservation)
- » 3 vanilla beans (mental powers, calm, passion)

Fill the bottle halfway with rum.

Cut the vanilla beans in half lengthwise and scrape out vanilla seeds.
Add seeds and pod to the potion.

Fill the jar the rest of the way with rum. Place in a cool, dark place.

Shake the bottle once a day for the first week.

Allow 6–8 weeks before use.

No need to remove the vanilla bean.

If you choose to remove the pod, consider adding it to your sugar bowl to give the sugar a mild vanilla flavor.

Some homemade recipes will tell you to use vodka since it is a neutral spirit; however, it is too neutral. Using whiskey or rum adds a dimension to the flavor that doesn't come with a vodka base. The oak aging already adds a vanilla note; the actual beans further develop the character without it ever tasting fake or overdone.

TEA-INFUSED VODKA

Vodka is a neutral base to enhance the flavors of any given material. Vodka allows the woods in oak barrels, conifers, and teas to bring those flavors to the surface in a way that steeping in water alone cannot replicate. Hot water does not have the chemical process *oomph* needed to break down the bark and allow the flavor to come out. Rooibos and honeybush tea both have leaves and bark to flavor vodka with a mild vanilla-like character.

Add ½ cup of desired tea leaves to sixteen ounces of 100 proof vodka. Permit yourself to experiment. Use the cheap vodka so you don't feel bad if it doesn't work out the way you'd like. Keep in a cool, dark place for 6–8 weeks before tasting. If you aren't a fan of the flavor you create, turn to the section on tea magic and use it in your intention work.

Tarot Time Tea Vodka

Tools

» Large bottle

Ingredients

» ½ cup honeybush tea—unflavored or vanilla (health, vitality, energy)

» 1 tsp. lavender buds—Hungarian or French, not English, it'll have a spicier flavor and doesn't run the risk of tasting soapy if left to macerate over-long (balance, harmony, peace, centering, protection)

» 16 oz. 100 proof vodka (security, money, health)

Blend all ingredients in the bottle.

Place in cool, dark cabinet 6–8 weeks before use.

Strain out the tea leaves and lavender.

Feel free to reuse the original bottle for storage.

Add to cocktails calling for vodka, that pair best with a soft flavor and calm spirit.

Please see Tarot Time Spritzer, page 175.

Peppermint-Infused Vodka

Tools

» 16 oz. bottle

Ingredients

» ¼ cup dried mint or ½ cup fresh

» Vodka

If using fresh mint (either from the produce aisle or the garden), hold mint by the base of the stems and slap it on the counter 2–3 times. This will bruise the leaves without adding chlorophyll (and green color) to your drink. Add peppermint to bottle, and pour vodka over the mint. Let stand 6–8 weeks before straining. Consider using this for making bitters as well!

Please see Hex-Breaking Mint and Grapefruit Tonic with Rosemary Syrup, page 176.

MAKE YOUR OWN BITTERS

Small-batch, niche bitters are pricey, potentially costing over twenty dollars per bottle. Making them yourself not only allows you to express yourself magically and artisanally, but it will also enable you to save time and money. With the number of tinctures on hand in many a witch's cabinets, it makes sense to give this a shot. The blending of tinctures is a quick and easy way to create bitters at home. The more delicate and time-intensive method is to blend all of the botanicals into one jar and tincture the blend itself. Starting with tinctures you've already created gives you a little more instant gratification.

Firstly, what's a tincture? A tincture is a base alcohol (usually vodka) with botanicals infused therein. The Peppermint-Infused Vodka? Tincture. The Tarot Time Tea Vodka? Tincture. The vodka breaks the cell walls of the botanicals and allows the flavors (also water and sugars, in the cases of fruit) to permeate the liquor. For further control, tincturing one material at a time in the same jar might be beneficial.

Once the materials have attained the flavor desired, sugar and water are added to sweeten the brew. Tinctures tend to be 100 proof, whereas the bitters that result should be around 90 proof. We're just adding enough simple syrup or honey to calm the bitters. (As I've said elsewhere, I don't recommend grain alcohol because of the cell damage it does.)

A tincture is 1 part botanical to 4 parts alcohol. For example, 1 ounce orange zest strips (or ¼ ounce oleosaccharum!) to 4 ounces vodka. Leave as much pith behind as possible. Rosemary makes a gorgeous tincture that captures the full range of scents available from wood and leaves. Strawberries are a lovely fruit to tincture because there usually are plenty on hand, and the tincture captures the flavor for the offseason. Chop finely, but don't muddle, or it will be difficult to strain back out. Steep soft fruit for a few days; the full flavor will be developed at 2 weeks. For dried herbs, bark, or seeds you will need 6–8 weeks. Citrus fruit zest can be ready in a day or two.

For blending bitters, I suggest 2-ounce amber glass bottles with droppers. To make bitters, I always buy the middle-of-the-road vodka. If I'm making medicinal tinctures (where only a few drops are ingested) cheaper is fine. Those don't need to taste good. I also use the "engine degreaser" grade vodka for floor washes.

Bitters get their name from the bitter herbs that flavor the blends, giving alcoholic beverages flavor and depth, and balancing sweetness. Gentian is the traditional bitter herb; Angostura bitters are made with gentian.

The magic of gentian is that of Venus. The associations for gentian are desire, lust, love, and pain. It increases the magical power of potions and brews with just a dash or two. It is the protection of our fiercest allies and the realization of practical knowledge. For magic in abating a chronic illness, or recovering from a lengthy one, enclose a piece of gentian root in a red cloth and carry on your person.

Gentian Bitters

Tools

» A 12 or 16 oz. bottle—as roots, barks, and woods swell when submerged

Ingredients

» 8 oz. 100 proof vodka

» 1 oz. gentian root

» 1 oz. simple syrup

Add gentian and vodka to the bottle. Let sit in a cool, dark place for 6–8 weeks. Shake the bottle every day for the first week to encourage flavoring. After the flavor has matured, strain out the root and add the simple syrup to the tincture. This recipe makes a *lot* of bitters, considering it is usually used a drop or two at a time in drinks. Fill the 2-ounce bottles with droppers and keep in the bar or make a decorative label and give as a gift.

Other bitter herbs for the base:

» Allspice berries (victory over an opponent)

» Angelica root (acceptance, gain, success, processing grief, protection)

» Apple peels (love, lust, fertility)

» Artemisia (psychic power, antianxiety, aphrodisiac)

» Artichoke leaf (banishing, love, lust, sex)

» Burdock root (protection, power, health, cleansing)

» Cassia (money, protection)

» Cherry bark or stones (happiness)

» Cinnamon sticks (purification, protection, prosperity)

» Coarse-ground coffee (prosperity, fertility, money)

Consider adding a flavoring agent to make it your own.

» Coriander (thought, intention, problem-solving)

» Dandelion root (strength, healing, divination)

» Lemon peel (purification, love)

» Lemongrass (fidelity, honesty, protection, calm)

» Orange peel (love, attraction, strength, prosperity)

» Orris root (love, lust, beauty)

» Peppercorns (protection, purification, thought, physical action)

- » Spicebush berries (purification, protection)
- » Wormwood (trance work, other planes, health)

Start with your bitter botanicals, choose your flavoring agents, and go play!

MAKE YOUR OWN VERMOUTH

Vermouth is a dry white wine that has been fortified with botanicals and brandy then sweetened.

Botanicals commonly used:

- » Angelica (acceptance, gain, success, processing grief, protection)
- » Bay (ancestor worship, attraction, endings, harmony, hex breaking)
- » Black peppercorns (protection, purification, thought, physical action)
- » Calamus (commanding, love, peace, balance)
- » Chamomile (banishing, luck, balancing aura, love, psychic dreams)
- » Cinnamon (purification, protection, prosperity)
- » Cloves (hex breaking, dispelling negative energy, protection)
- » Coriander (clairvoyance, divination, healing, retention, secrets)
- » Fennel (protection, healing, purification, warding the home)
- » Ginger (energizing, love, healing, power, money, magical strength)
- » Grains of paradise (protection, wealth, luck)
- » Juniper (talents, protection, dreams, fertility, new abilities)
- » Marjoram (keeping away harmful people, protection, love, money)
- » Myrrh (meditation, peace, fertility, progress, release, spirituality)
- » Orange peel (love, attraction, strength, prosperity)
- » Rosemary (character, courage, wisdom, uplifting, purification)
- » Sage (cleansing, protection)

» Star anise (love, fidelity)

» Vanilla—bean and pod (passion, relaxation)

» Wormwood (binding, psychic stimulation, elemental magic)

Blend botanicals until fragrant and delightful. It is essential that you enjoy the smell of the blended herbs, because the magic will speak to you, and you'll be more likely to use and enjoy it if it starts off smelling good. Once you have a blend that smells appealing to you, you'll need one cup of the dried botanical blend. Note: make sure to write down the herbs you used and a rough guess at how much of each, so you can recreate it if you fall in love.

Vermouth

Tools

» Small pot with lid

» Small saucepan

» Cookie sheet

» Parchment paper

» Cheesecloth

» Wire strainer

» Bowl

Ingredients

» 1 bottle dry white wine (devotion, spirituality, accomplishments)

» 2 cups sugar (love)

» 1 cup herbal blend

» ⅔ cup brandy (ecstasy, overcoming self-consciousness)

Allow 1½ cups white wine to simmer with 1 cup sugar and 1 cup herbal mixture for 10 minutes. Do not boil. Make sure to put the lid on; we don't want all of those precious volatile oils being lost to the air. After 10 minutes, remove from heat and allow to sit for an additional 22 minutes.

Place the remaining cup of sugar into a small saucepan with 4 tbsp. water—just barely enough water to partially dissolve it. Turn the heat on high and gently swirl the sugar/water mixture. Don't over stir; we want the sugar to caramelize, without burning. Cook until thickened and ready to pour. Place a sheet or two of parchment paper onto a cookie sheet, pour the caramel onto it, and set aside to cool. Tip: place the baking sheet onto a cooling rack so that the counter doesn't hold in the heat and lengthen your set time.

After 20 minutes have passed, place a bowl on the counter to catch the liquid and cover a wire strainer with two layers of cheesecloth. Pour the liquid through the strainer and into the bowl. After it has mostly drained, pull up the ends of the cheesecloth and wring by hand to get more liquid out. Feel free to compost the herbs when you're done. Once the caramel is cool to the touch (try the bottom of the pan first; don't burn yourself), break it into small pieces and place back in the saucepan. Pour infused liquid over the caramel, cover, and heat on low until caramel dissolves. Then pour into a 1000 ml bottle, and top with remaining white wine. Cap the bottle, give it a shake, and then label it. Store in the refrigerator for up to three months. Enjoy homemade vermouth with cucumber water, seltzer, or added to vodka for a martini. It is also delightful by itself on a hot summer night.

COCKTAIL RECIPES

Witch's Poinsettia Punch

Tools

- » Patterned Bundt™ pan
- » Punch bowl

Ingredients

- » 1 lb. cranberries (healing, inspiration, protection, release tension)
- » 1 bottle spumante, Moscato, or other sweet sparkling wine (fertility, prosperity, devotional, inspiration)
- » 3 cups cranberry juice cocktail (protection, release, inspiration)
- » 1 cup Cranberry-Infused Triple Sec, strained—see page 161 for recipe (love, attraction, beauty, fidelity, happiness, sensuality)
- » Optional: sugar
- » Optional: orange

Day of event (T-minus 4 hours to party time)

Take ¾–1 lb. of cranberries and pour them into the Bundt pan. Add 1 cup of cranberry juice cocktail and enough water to cover the berries by 1 inch, to the pan. Place in the freezer.

Day of event (T-minus 30 minutes to party time)

Take cake pan from the freezer and run the outside of the pan under lukewarm water. This will help the ice ring release from the mold. Place ice ring in the punch bowl. To the punch bowl, add 1 large bottle of sweet, sparkling wine, 3 cups of cranberry juice cocktail, and 1 cup of the flavored triple sec. Add orange slices and any remaining cranberries for garnish if desired. This blend of fruits inspires love and camaraderie, allows guests to celebrate their accomplishments, and releases tension for a smoothly flowing party atmosphere.

Post-Holiday Slump Spritz

Tools

- » Glass
- » Spoon

Ingredients

- » 1 oz. Pine-Infused Vodka—see page 161 for recipe
- » 7 oz. ginger beer or ale (healing, energy, courage, luck)
- » Ice

Stir gently, then garnish with a lemon twist.

Visualize your intended goal while sipping and feel your spirits rise as you enjoy the aromatic benefit of pine as well as the sweet enjoyment of the ginger.

Werewolves of London Martini Tea Cocktail

Tools

- » Martini glass
- » Tea infuser
- » Cocktail shaker

Ingredients

- » Ice
- » 2½ tsp. Earl Grey tea (green Earl Grey is best) (commanding, attraction, money)
- » 1 oz. preferred dry gin—the brand Bombay® Dry Gin is especially lovely with this (enabling action; protection from ghosts, harm, and

evil) or use Earl Grey Tea-Infused Gin for an extra kick of bergamot and tea flavor—see page 162 for recipe

» 4 oz. water (175° for green tea, 195° for black tea)

» Lavender syrup—from Chapter 8 (centering, peace, balance, protection)

Chill a martini glass with ice during preparation.

Boil water and cool to the desired temperature.

Add tea to the infuser and pour the hot water over it.

Steep 2 minutes for green tea, 4 minutes for black tea.

Remove tea leaves.

Pour over ice in a cocktail shaker.

Add gin and lavender syrup.

Shake.

Strain into chilled glass.

Love Lies Bleeding Cocktail

Tools

» Cocktail shaker

» Highball glass

Ingredients

» 1 oz. Vanilla and Cinnamon-Infused Whiskey—see page 162 (growth, abundance, calm, love)

» 1 oz. Amaretto (creativity, defense, love, passion, open mind)

» ½ oz. sloe gin (banishing, binding, destiny, fidelity, ending problems)

» 1 oz. fresh apple juice (love, attraction, beauty, strength, happiness)

Add all ingredients to a cocktail shaker, then add ice.

Shake the cocktail shaker vigorously while sending intention to liquid.

Strain into a high ball glass filled with ice.

This take on an Alabama Slammer is filled with loving and invigorating ingredients inspired to bring love into your life.

Tarot Time Spritzer

Tools

- » Heavy-bottomed glass
- » Muddler

Ingredients

- » 8 oz. sparkling water
- » 1 oz. Tarot Time Tea Vodka—see page 165
- » 1 tsp. simple syrup
- » ½ cup strawberries, diced
- » Ice
- » Sparkling water

Add simple syrup to the glass.

Pour in diced strawberries and vodka.

Muddle.

Add a handful of ice cubes.

Top with sparkling water and stir gently.

This strawberries-and-cream styled drink is superb in summer at cooling the heat, but in winter, it's a divine reminder of warmer times.

Hex-Breaking Mint and Grapefruit Tonic with Rosemary Syrup

Tools

- » Cocktail shaker
- » Highball glass

Ingredients

- » 4 oz. tonic (stimulating)
- » 2 oz. grapefruit juice (healing, self-esteem, protection, renewal, focus)
- » 1 oz. Rosemary Syrup—see page 186 (happiness, hex breaking, protection, purification)
- » 1 oz. Peppermint-Infused Vodka—see page 165 (action, alertness, clarity, release, purification)
- » Ice

To a cocktail shaker, add vodka, grapefruit juice, and rosemary syrup. Top with ice and shake vigorously imagining any hexes or ill will burning away.

Strain into a highball glass, top with tonic, and garnish with a mint sprig.

Drink to your (magical) health.

Fruit Feeling Frisky

Now that we have talked about the magic found in the kitchen and the bar, let us talk about some things that can be used in both places.

SWITCHEL

Switchel is as old as the sea, it seems. There are references to Ruth drinking a vinegar-based beverage while working in the fields of Boaz in the Bible (Ruth 2:14). Edwardian and Elizabethan eras saw a rise in nostalgia, claiming a Classical Greek and Roman heyday of the family of beverages, but there isn't a historical record supporting that. Switchel is a blend of water, vinegar, and molasses. Long ago, it was prescribed to pirates at sea when potable water was questionable at best. Vinegar kept the down the harmful bacteria and fungus. Romantic notions of drunken pirates on grog always have a kernel of truth. However, alcoholic beverages (even watered-down ones) can be dangerous in rising temperatures when physical labor is needed. Switchel, a cooling beverage, is credited with bringing down fevers.

Switchel is very easy to make. All that is required is water, vinegar, and sweetener. Using ingredients like apple cider vinegar that contains Mother (the SCOBY used in the second fermentation of the vinegar) is reputed to have health benefits from the probiotics. It contains three ingredients to start with, but where you go after that is up to your imagination.

One popular switchel was Haymaker's Punch, which was kept on hand in fields during the harvest. It was flavored with molasses, which was cheap and plentiful.

Haymaker's Punch

Tools

- » Saucepan
- » Whisk
- » Sterilized bottles

Ingredients

- » 1 gallon water
- » 1½ cups molasses
- » ½ cup apple cider vinegar
- » Optional: the juice of one lemon, lime, or other citrus fruit

Warm the water in a saucepan while whisking molasses into water. Stir continually while heating water over low heat. Once incorporated fully, turn off the heat and allow it to cool.

Once the molasses water is cooled to room temperature, stir in apple cider vinegar, pour into sterilized bottles, and place them in the refrigerator to chill. The cooling action of the switchel should feel refreshing in your mouth, rather than cloying. If it feels heavy on the tongue, reduce the amount of sweetener in the next batch.

A note about apple cider vinegar: It stands to reason that this vinegar is made from apple cider, so what keeps the vinegar from becoming cyser or fermented cider over time? The answer is much like any great discovery: an accident. *Acetobacter* species bacteria would contaminate containers meant for cyser during the secondary fermentation. Upon opening the bottle and hoping to find fermented cider, they would discover vinegar, similarly to the way red wine vinegar happens. Now, acetobacter bacteria is intentionally added to the containers so that vinegar is more intentional. The bacterial colony that forms in the tank can reproduce and be used to make additional batches, similarly to kombucha (see Chapter 6).

THE MAGIC OF SWITCHEL

» The magic of this delectable drink cannot be overstated. All fermented substances can be used for transformational magic.

» Apples are associated with Venus, Iðunn, and other goddesses of love, as well as youthfulness, lust, and fertility.

» Sweeteners like honey, molasses, and agave have been used to sweeten the disposition of lovers, bosses, family, and more from time immemorial. Sweetening jars are filled with honey, photos of the intended, and herbs before being closed, and candles are burned on the lid to sweeten temperaments with much success.

To sweeten temperaments in the home or office, serve a refreshing pitcher of ginger and lemon switchel at a summer picnic, or ginger and clove to ward off colds and flu. It is easy to explain away the drink as you wanting to "keep the office healthy." The health benefits of apple cider vinegar are reputed to include keeping the immune system primed. You and I will know that all the sweetener has been charmed with your intent to calm tempers and soothe egos, too.

Summertime Cool-Down Switchel

Tools

» Saucepan

» Pitcher

Ingredients

» 1 thumb ginger, chopped

» 4 cups water

» 1 cup local honey—if you commute to work, try to find local honey closer to the office; learn more about honey in Chapter 9.

» 1 cup apple cider vinegar—with Mother if you want probiotic benefits

» Juice of 1 lemon—about 4 tbs.

Chop ginger into chunks and add to saucepan with water.

Bring the water to a boil, and boil for 5 minutes. This is called a *decoction* when you boil roots and barks that are too hard to make as a *tisane*. While heating, stir in honey until dissolved. Once it has boiled for 5 minutes, remove from heat and cool to room temperature.

Scoop out the ginger. If you're making a Ginger Bug (see page 151), toss the sugary ginger into the fermenting crock, if not compost.

Once this mixture is cooled, stir in the vinegar. If the water is too hot when you toss in the vinegar, it will kill off the beneficial bacteria. Add the lemon juice. Place in a pitcher and cool.

Lemon's bright scent is calming, reassuring, and mood lifting. In magic, lemon is used to increase a spell's power. It has also been used for love, mental clarity, purification, and banishing fatigue.

Winter Warm-Up Switchel

Tools

» Saucepan

» Pitcher

Ingredients

» 4 cups water

- » 1 thumb ginger, chopped
- » 1 cup local honey—if you commute to work, try to find local honey closer to the office; more about honey in this chapter
- » 1 cup apple cider vinegar—with Mother if you want probiotic benefits
- » 1 teaspoon whole cloves

Chop ginger into chunks and add to saucepan with water.

Bring the water to a boil, and boil for 5 minutes. While heating, stir in honey until dissolved. Once it has boiled for 5 minutes, remove from heat and allow to cool to room temperature.

Scoop out ginger. See previous recipe for more information.

Once this mixture is cooled, stir in the vinegar. If the water is too hot when you toss in the vinegar, it will kill off the beneficial bacteria. Place in a pitcher and cool.

SHRUBS

Fruit is that delectably sweet and natural joy that grows right in the ground. These seasonal delights come into our lives for a short time each year and vanish just as quickly as they arrived. Even with the advent of modern grocery stores extending the growing season artificially by bringing fruits and vegetables from outside the area, it never is quite the same. The long-distance fruit-like strawberries are commonly gas ripened because they were picked when they were still green, to have as much shelf life as possible.

Various climates around the world led to the adoption of preservation methods to keep these bright flavors around as long as possible. These preservation methods meant that fruit could be used for far longer than otherwise likely. Drying, canning, and other methods were dependent on the weather, available supply, and many other factors. If you were drying fruit (usually with high water content) and the movement of the air stopped, it could lead to molding, ruining the entire batch. Beverages are what we will concentrate on here. Canning does not seem worth it with a small harvest, as it is a labor-intensive job, usually when the year is the hottest.

Shrubs are sweetened vinegar drinks based on fruits and vegetables and flavored with herbs. From the Arabic word *to drink*, shrubs were a favorite in the early Colonial period (1700s) for the readily available ingredients. They also could save fruits and vegetables from waste, and the cooling effect on the body was handy before air conditioning was invented. By adding the fruit to the switchel base, shrubs have an infinite blend of flavors available and are excellent for fruit that is near spoiling. Rotten spots can be cut out during the preparation phase, and the vinegar breaks the cell wall of the organic matter to release much of the water content. A small amount of this syrup is then added to water, club soda, and other beverages to add dimension and flavor.

HOW TO MAKE YOUR SHRUB

1. Select the fruit. They don't have to be photo-worthy berries to be *tasty* when your shrub is finished. Wash them thoroughly before starting. Fruit like apples have a wax coating that is applied before shipping to grocery stores. Consider a wax-removing wash (or even pouring warm water over it to melt the wax). If you're worried about any of these methods, you can peel your apples, pears, and other fruit before slicing or chopping. Optional: pick out herbs to flavor your shrub, or make an herbal shrub next time. (My favorite is ginger and lavender.)

2. Stir it up. If it is a soft fruit, I love to give it a rough stir after chopping before I do anything else. If it is a hard material, pre-stirring the fruit won't make a difference. The ideal ratio for shrubs is 1:1:1, one part fruit to one part sugar to one part vinegar for the balance of sweet and tart.

3. Now, add the sweetener—sugar, honey, agave, molasses, whichever sweetener you prefer. (I have not experimented with artificial

sweeteners; your mileage may vary.) You will need one cup of sweetener per cup of fruit. Give it another stir and don't worry about bruising the fruit; the vinegar is going to do that for you. Feel free to give it a little mashing while you stir. Remember, every kind of sugar will add a different dimension to the shrub. White sugar will have a bright, high note to it. Honey will be softer and warmer, and agave will be very light on the palate so that it won't overpower a bright flavor like watermelon.

4. Add enough vinegar for the 1:1:1 ratio. Just as the sweeteners used will change the flavor of the shrub, try to match light characteristics with light vinegar, like Prosecco vinegar, apple cider vinegar, red wine, or white vinegar. For bold fruits, consider balsamic vinegar and other more substantial kinds of vinegar. If using balsamic, you can get a bold flavor with a little vinegar by adding cider vinegar to cut costs but not taste. Now is also the time to add herbs or spices if doing so. Remember, if using fresh instead of dried, double the amount required.

5. Let sit on a cool counter, covered with cheesecloth, overnight for as long as two days. Stir once a day.

6. Strain off the fruit. You can compost the fruit, use it to top your sodas, blend it into smoothies, or top ice cream with it.

7. Pour the remaining liquid into airtight, sterilized bottles.

For shrub sodas, pour ¼ cup syrup into a glass with ¾ cup soda water. Since the syrup is more substantial, it'll sink to the bottom and will need a gentle stir.

For adult beverages, use a 1:4 ratio of syrup to soda, or other mixers, plus your liquor of choice. Place the syrup and alcohol into a shaker to mix, pour over ice, and top with soda.

FAVORITE SHRUBS

» Strawberries, apple cider vinegar, and white sugar (happiness, friendship spells)

» Peaches, white vinegar, lavender, raw sugar (spells for romance and longevity)

» Watermelon, Prosecco vinegar, white sugar (healing spells)

» Strawberries, chocolate balsamic vinegar, raw sugar (loving relationship magic)

» Parsnips, carrots, white vinegar, maple sugar (love, sex, fertility magic)

» Strawberries, lemon vinegar, white sugar (magic protecting happiness)

There is a second method for making shrubs. Gently simmer fruit in simple syrup for a few hours. This method is recommended if leaving fruit in vinegar on the counter is ill-advised in your climate. After simmering, add the vinegar. Consider using flavored syrups to add another dimension to the flavor. A good rule to follow is that if the fruit is commonly preserved, it can be processed with the simmer method (strawberries, blueberries, cherries, and the like).

SYRUPS

Ginger Syrup

Tools

» Saucepan

» Sterilized bottles

Ingredients

- » 1 tsp. lemon zest (calm, clarity, love, friendship)
- » 2 cups ginger, sliced into coins (energizing, power, passion, money)
- » 4 cups sugar (banishing depression, love, sweetening a bad mood)
- » 4 cups water
- » Optional: vanilla bean (calming, passion, relaxing)

Since ginger is a hardened and fibrous root, boil the ginger on low in the syrup water for 10–15 minutes before stirring in the sugar, vanilla bean, and lemon zest last. Turn off the heat and let it cool to room temperature. You don't get burned, and it gives the syrup the maximum amount of time before removing the material. Compost the ginger, or julienne the boiled ginger slices and add to vodka (with the vanilla bean if you used it) for an infused mixer. (See Chapter 7 for more ideas.) Pour into sterilized bottles and refrigerate for up to 2 weeks.

Homemade Ginger Ale: 2 oz. Ginger Syrup to 6 oz. club soda.

Ginger Magic: Health, healing, courage, energizing, magical strength, power, and prosperity.

Lavender Syrup

Tools

- » Saucepan
- » Bottle or jar

Ingredients

- » 2 cups sugar
- » 2 cups water
- » 2 tsp. dried lavender buds

Bring water to a boil, turn off heat, and stir in the sugar.

Continue to stir until clear.

Add lavender flowers and allow it to cool to room temperature.

Strain and bottle. Keep in the refrigerator for up to 1 month.

Add to Earl Grey tea with milk for a lavender London Fog tea latte. Bergamot is the energy of success, and lavender is calming, so it makes a perfect drink to take with you before a job interview!

Lavender Magic: Secrets, balance, keeping things hidden, strength, love, mental stimulant, psychic development, gentleness, divination, clairvoyance, centering, peace, calming, protection, harmony.

Rosemary Syrup

Tools

- » Saucepan
- » Sterilized bottles

Ingredients

- » 1 cup rosemary leaves and branches (character, confidence, release, strength, wisdom)
- » 2 cups sugar (banishing depression, love, sweetening a bad mood)
- » 2 cups water
- » Optional: vanilla bean (calm, passion, relaxing)

Rosemary is a woody plant, so rather than pouring boiling water over the stems, we must boil water and then simmer the branches on low in the water for 10–15 minutes. Turn off the heat. Let it cool to room temperature. You don't get burned, and it gives the syrup the maximum amount of flavor before removing the material. Compost the rosemary, or add to vodka for an infused mixer. Pour into sterilized bottles and refrigerate for up to 2 weeks. Add Tarot Time Tea Vodka for a vanilla flavoring and extended shelf life.

OLEOSACCHARUM

Picture it—the sun is shining, and all is right with the world. You reach for an orange on the kitchen table and start to peel it. Rip, the orange peel tears, and the pores of the orange explode into a perfect citrus mist, perfuming the entire kitchen. Bartenders and mixologists everywhere know the secret to adding this gorgeous scent and flavor to their concoctions. The final step in making an old-fashioned is to express the orange peel over the glass and drop in the twist. To get the brightness of citrus into vintage punch recipes, they called for a syrup named oleosaccharum. This "oil sugar" was created as another way of using all of the fruit. When citrus peels are coated with sugar and left on the counter, the sugar starts to break down and extract the oil in the peel, without adding water. This concept is readily demonstrated in the summer months when strawberries are ripe and plentiful. When strawberries are diced and sprinkled with sugar, the bowl starts to accumulate a delicious strawberry syrup in the bottom of the bowl. When your oleosaccharum is complete, you have a brightly colored, aromatic syrup that packs a punch.

Oleosaccharum (this is more of a suggestion)

Tools

- » Mixing bowl—glass works best because it is a nonreactive material
- » Citrus peeler

Ingredients

- » 2 grapefruits (healing, protection, self-esteem, joy)
- » 8 tangerines or 4 large oranges (abundance, confidence, change)
- » ¾ cup of sugar (banishing depression, love, lust, preservation)

Peel the fruit, leaving as much pith behind as possible. Pith makes your brews bitter. Sprinkle sugar over the peels and stir. Make sure to coat as much of the citrus peel as possible. Cover with a tea towel and leave on the counter for 4–24 hours depending on strength desired. It will get stronger the longer it sits out. Strain and bottle in an airtight container and refrigerate. Good refrigerated for up to a week.

Love Potion, Chapter 9:
Tea and Honey Magic

THE MAGICAL USES OF TEA

I started blending my own magical teas fifteen years ago. As a child, some of the first "magic" I encountered was my mom making sweet tea for our family. She looked like an alchemist to my young eyes. She made her own simple syrup, and I can still see her knotting the handful of teabags together for ease of retrieval. She was turning plain water into the magical brew our family enjoyed with meals, when returning home from school, or on a hot day. I couldn't wait to make my own tea for my loved ones. There are days that I credit that day as the day my magical tea shop was born.

WHAT IS TEA?

Tea is a plant that grows in China, India, and the American south. The teas that we commonly associate with our ritual *cuppa* all come from the same plant, the *Camellia sinensis*. It was reputedly discovered by the Chinese emperor Shen-nong, who found the herb in 2737 BCE. The story goes that he was boiling water outside, and a leaf of the *Camellia sinensis* fell into his pot. He sipped the water and was entranced with the flavor and energy it gave him.

Keep in mind that not everything that is called tea really is. Herbs and botanicals that aren't *Camellia sinensis* and are made in hot water are called tisanes. A tisane can be honeybush with cinnamon, or a cup of chamomile with honey after a long day.

TEA AND WITCHCRAFT

Incorporating tea into your magical practice has a long history and blends two well-known disciplines: plant magic and divination. Tea is a plant of transformation with so many varieties and preparations that perform so many unique magical tasks. Though all tea comes from the same plant, the growing environment plays a large part in the outcome of the tea, as do the methods of drying and variety of the plant. The tea plant is so delicate that the leaves pick up the aromas of the environment in which they are grown. Hawaiian tea tastes vastly different from Chinese tea because, in Hawaii, the tea farms are likely very close to the other major crop of Hawaii, pineapple. Merely having the scent of fresh pineapple on the air allows these leaves to mature and retain a hint of their pineapple neighbors.

White tea is comprised of the young leaves that are picked before they reach maturity. It has a delicate flavor and is easily "overcooked" as a drink. For a cup of white tea, you'll need 1½ teaspoons of dried tea leaves, water that is 175°, and once water is added, it will need to steep for between 4 and 5 minutes. Having water too hot or leaving the leaves in too long will result in a bitter brew.

White tea is associated with spring's new buds and the explosion of color, fertility, and life. The magic of white tea is that of purification, aura cleansing, prosperity, fecundity, psychic protection, and abundance. It makes an excellent offering to various gods as it blesses and fosters connection with others, including beneficial spirits. It can bring clarity to any issue. The youth of the tea leaves forges a bond with beginnings, beauty, and childhood.

Green tea arises from the dried mature leaves of the tea plant. A proper cup of green tea uses 1 teaspoon of dried leaves, water that is 175°, and is steeped for only 1–2 minutes. A great many people think that green tea is too bitter or grassy for them to enjoy, but that is usually due to an improperly prepared cup. Green tea has a soft, vegetative flavor that is delicate and pairs well with fruits, especially citrus. Green tea is associated with the magic of summer. Ginseng green tea is useful for banishing nightmares. Note: When a mild caffeination is mentioned for green tea, it is not matcha that is being discussed. Matcha is a green tea, but with matcha, the entire green tea leaf is powdered and consumed, meaning that all of the caffeine inherent in the leaf is consumed. Matcha has three to four times the amount of caffeine of brewed green tea.

Magically, green tea is used for abundance, the same color as fertile grounds in the spring. Green tea's antioxidants and a moderate amount of caffeine connect it to heath and long life. That small amount of caffeine lends itself well to harnessing energy for spells that banish negative energies. The tea can be brewed and used to asperge and cleanse a home or workplace. Green tea is also an aphrodisiac used in love spells where the mild caffeination can improve circulation to vital areas.

Oolong tea is a partially withered tea that is mildly caffeinated and has a soothing flavor, somewhere between a green and black tea. In magic it is associated with the fall because it is the bridge between the summery green tea and rich black tea. Oolong tea has associations of peace, the inner examination of the self, divination, centering emotions, and affection. Oolong tea is brewed like a black tea, using 1 teaspoon of tea in 195° water for 3–4 minutes.

The magical action of Oolong tea is that of love because it represents the marriage of the black tea and the green tea. The ritual of brewing the tea leaves time for meditation and inner thought, so working magic for these aims is appropriate while brewing. The balance of green and black tea leaves also makes it the perfect tea for finding balance in our minds and hearts.

Black tea is made by fermenting green tea leaves in water for long periods of time. The longer the fermentation, the more significant the amount of caffeine. In the mountains of China where black tea was born, the tea leaves would be picked, placed in a vat filled with water, and left in caves near where the tea was grown. Black tea is best enjoyed by brewing 1 teaspoon tea in water at 195° for 3–4 minutes.

In magic, black tea is useful because it can banish feelings, apathy, sleepiness, and directionlessness. The higher caffeine content leads to feelings of bravery, freedom from boredom, and a sense of adventure and expansive thought. As with other stimulating substances like cinnamon, clove, and cardamom, black tea can be beneficial for prosperity as well.

Rooibos tea (*Aspalathus linearis*) gets its name meaning "red tea" from the appearance of the plant. The honeybush tea (*Cyclopia intermedia*), named after the honey-like fragrance of the flowers, was mostly unknown to the world outside of South Africa until 2001. In 2001 The Republic of Tea tea company started basing teas on this flavorful, antioxidant-rich family of leaves. Rooibos is left on the plant to ripen and fall off the plants and oxidize in the sun. Conversely, with green rooibos the younger leaves are not allowed to oxidize, and they retain a sweeter flavor. These dark red-brown botanicals have a very mild fruity flavor and do not get bitter if over-steeped. Both plants are also drought tolerant. For brewing use 1½ teaspoons of tea in water at 208° for 5–6 minutes.

The tea itself has many healthful associations magically and makes an excellent base for tea in tea-leaf reading. Those earthy energies also make it suitable for teas invoking motherly energy, fertility, prosperity, grounding, health, and nurturing.

CHARGING YOUR TEA WITH INTENT

To turn your cup of tea into a potion, you just add magic! Whether you're using loose-leaf teas or a tea bag, the intention has to be applied. Decide on a goal. Make sure it is appropriately worded in the positive. Center your purpose in your mind. "I am going to pass my English final." Gather intent and power into the palms of your hands, and use the energy to charge the tea leaves. Pour your hot water over the leaves and allow the heat of the water to charge your brew. Remove the tea after the correct steep time, and add sugar and cream as you like. Enjoy, continuing to visualize your intended outcome.

DESIGNING A TEA SPELL

To create your own magical tea, there are a few steps to consider. Once you have the idea, experiment. Keep making, keep blending those teas. The only way you master something is by doing it. Research is lovely (and necessary), but is no replacement for getting your hands in there. Tip: Many tea shops have 1- or 2-ounce containers of loose tea leaves. With these smaller containers, you can purchase several types and flavors of tea to experiment with.

Step 1: What is your goal?
Not every tea blend needs to be magical. Sometimes the goal is just to get your family to drink something other than a canned soda. It can be as intricate as you wish. Remember, every material that goes into your potion is magical; it is the intent that powers that spell.

As a witch, traveling from shop to shop for over twenty years, I've seen my share of magical teas. I was often disappointed at the selection. Sometimes they were actually beneficial herbal teas for one ailment or another. Still, they had been placed in a clear plastic baggie and left to hang in the sunny window for years until they became dusty relics with no discernible flavor or color.

So, is your goal to bring harmony to your household? Is it to have the energy to finish a project on time? Is your aim to relax after a stressful day? Deciding on the intended outcome not only cements the magic in your mind, but it also helps inform the choices you make for the rest of the work. If your goal is to de-stress after a stressful day at work, you might not pick a high caffeine base like Maté. If you need quick cash, you might not pick only fruits associated with love.

Step 2: Grab a notebook!

When working out this process, I find it helpful to write it out. It puts all of the options out there and makes it easy to recreate blends that are a) effective and b) tasty!

Write down all of the things you associate with your goal. This is the free-form, brainstorming portion of the exercise. Looking at your thoughts on paper can allow you to make connections you might otherwise have missed.

Money:

» Almond

» Basil

» Bergamot

» Cedar

» Clary sage

» Clove

» Lemon

» Orange

» Patchouli

» Strawberry

» Tangerine

Step 3: Look at correspondences.

This list obviously has things in it that maybe wouldn't taste all that great, or don't agree with you for reasons of preference or allergies. Listen to the preference as much as you would allergies. If you have an aversion to rose petals because of allergies (me), it is as valid as having a traumatic memory of oranges. Our society tells people that they need to just get over their trauma without really understanding what that means. Yes, there is a way to deal with aversions to ingredients for associative reasons, but that's a story for another book. The simple fact is that if you genuinely object to something and decide to push the issue and include it in your working, a) you won't want to drink it and will avoid the working because of it, and b) if you make yourself do it anyway, your magic is going to be blocked because you are rejecting an ingredient therein. It's much easier and psychically gentle to pick something else and examine your feelings in a neutral place at a different time.

Looking at this list there are a few tea options I can see. Almond is associated with abundance, fortune, money, wisdom, and prosperity and each of those things adds a different flavor (pardon the pun) to the magic it offers your tea. Looking at the additional correspondences can help us add more specific help to the tea. Almond is also associated with beauty, communication, consecration, peace, and joy. It's the attributes that aren't specifically geared toward money that can tell you the most about the kind of prosperity tea almond could make. An almond-based prosperity tea would be one that encourages spiritual growth, joy, and long-term budgeting. Fast cash disappears as fast as it comes into the picture, so adding a woody, stable element to that tea will root the prosperity in the long term.

Basil is an interesting addition to this list. I could see pairing basil and almond together. Basil will clear the mind of the past issues with money, giving a clean slate. It is stimulating for the mind, so it can help spot solutions for problems as well as making sure money woes aren't causing sleep disturbances.

Since this tea hopes to stimulate the situation, black tea is an excellent choice.

Obviously, if you are sensitive to caffeine avoid the black tea. Reminder: decaffeinated doesn't mean zero caffeine, it means less caffeine. Rooibos tea and honeybush tea are plants native to South Africa and produce a caffeine-free tea base with a mellow flavor. In the case of a caffeine issue, I'd add a stimulating plant to my rooibos base, like cinnamon to a plant associated with fertility, like dried apple.

Step 4: Smell a few combinations.
Before starting to blend, smell a small amount of your intended materials together. For this, I use custard cups in the kitchen. If my pieces don't work well together, I can put them back into their containers without contamination. Nothing is wasted. The reason I don't smell the large canisters at the same time is that each one has a different amount in it and will have different strength scents, where equal amounts are a better measure of how they will taste together.

Step 5: Make sure you are writing down your findings.
The thoughts that go through your head while blending and sampling should be recorded so you can more easily recall the smells, combinations, and features of each for future creations. Just because strawberry and lemon work well together doesn't mean they are suited to your immediate need for a money spell. They might be more suited to attracting a faithful and loving partner in a later tea.

My favorite tea from a magical shop was Fruit Paradise from Bell, Book, and Candle in Baltimore, Maryland, in 1999. Sadly, that tin didn't have any ingredients listed, so no matter how hard I tried, fifteen years later, I still couldn't recapture that sweet berry flavor.

Step 6: Blend your tea!
Start with equal parts of each material in the initial blending so it is easier to figure out whether it needs more or less of a certain ingredient. Keep in mind that woody materials need more heat over a longer

period of time to release their highest potential. They will continue to release their flavor as long as they are in the teacup. Leaving something containing clove, for instance, can quickly overpower a more delicate brew if allowed to steep too long.

Step 7: Add water!

Once you think you have the perfect ratio, write it down—something like "Test batch #1." Remember to be as detailed as possible. If you like "x" ingredient, but "y" ingredient is too powerful a flavor, you should be able to try a lesser amount for a more ideal blend. Blend a teaspoon to a teaspoon and a half of the experimental brew with water and see how it reacts. Try it without sweetener, then try it with. Try it with creamer or your favorite cream substitute.

Step 8: Evaluate.

Think of what you liked and didn't like. Not every tea is going to be a winner. There will be things you adore and things that have their place. Not every person will like everything you create, even your favorite ones. That's okay. For now, just blend for you. You can take over the world tomorrow.

Step 9: Capture your tea.

The choice between loose-leaf and tea bags is an old one. With loose-leaf tea, you can see every glorious ingredient. With tea bags, you get a quick and convenient solution to all your tea hopes. Is there a middle ground? Fillable tea bags (also called tea filters) are a popular solution to this issue. They allow the tea to breathe and infuse properly. Do-it-yourself sealable tea bags allow you to control how strong your brew is and what goes into your bags. Tea infusers are coming down in price and allow the tea to fully bloom and attain its best flavor, whereas tea balls can fall open, leak leaves out of the large water holes, and can burn your fingers when attempting to remove them from hot tea. All of these are things to consider when making longer-term tea choices. My suggestion is always tea infusers; they don't have the waste of teabags. I compost all my tea and my gardens love it. The tea gets to breathe and the mesh sieve is fine enough to catch even the smallest piece of honeybush bark.

Above all, label your tea. Whether you make up a name for it or just put the ingredients on a label, for the love of Pete, label everything.

Storing your tea

One of the most important things to consider when blending your magical tea is where to store it after you have created it. Now you may not need to store it. If you are mixing up the tea to be steeped and enjoyed at that moment, this is a moot point. But, proper storage of the blends you create will ensure that you get the best life out of your ingredients. It also means that when you go back for another cup, there will be more on hand. The three most important things to remember when storing tea:

*• **Block out light**—UV rays destroy the integrity of the ingredients and break down volatile oils that give your cherished blends a scent . . . and magic. They rob the tea of its color and structure. Due to this, there are companies that make UV-blocking tea containers, but they will specifically state that they are UV-blocking and they will cost a bit more.*

*• **Constant temperature**—Steep fluctuations in temperature can greatly reduce the shelf life of a tea as well. High temperatures can break down the volatile oils, and freezing temperatures can break down the plant matter anchoring those oils, making your tea crumble rather than unfurl.*

*• **Intercept oxygen**—Oxygen robs you of the smell of your teas, as the volatility of our materials is the rate at which their oils evaporate. Every molecule that evaporates is one less that adds to your taste, aroma, and experience. Airtight containers are the way to go.*

An enriching thought exercise in blending tea is to look up plants associated with the closest astrological planets. The newer planets, astrologically speaking, have fewer known associations, and many that are not potable or are poisonous. Pluto, for example, is a god of the underworld and rules over death, so it makes sense that the herbs associated with Him are poisonous.

Plants associated with Venus are:

» Apple

» Apricot

» Cardamom

» Lavender

» Peach

» Strawberry

» Vanilla

» Honey—not a plant, but still carries Her association

If you wanted to blend a tea in honor of Aphrodite, you could combine any of these in a way that sounded/smelled appealing. You might blend:

» Apples and apricot

» Peaches and cloves

» Vanilla and apple

You could add honeybush or rooibos base for a warm flavor and to give the tea some body.

THE MAGICAL USES OF HONEY

Sugar (derived from sugarcane) has the magic of unconditional love and sweetness between people. Honey has more specific attributions depending on the source plant. With honey, each flower will add a different flavor to the labor of the bees. Orange blossom honey will have a slight citrus note to the backside of the tongue, something you can almost smell rather than taste. Buckwheat honey will have a strong, almost smoky flavor with the air of wheat fields and works well if you plan to match it with bourbon, whiskey, or scotch. In the United States, the most commonly available honey is clover, but caveat emptor, beware most commercial jars of honey are watered down with rice sugar and other syrups and are rarely 100% real honey. Your best bet is to find a small batch supplier.

Every state in the United States has its own honey, as do most regions in the world. Each one lends a different profile. The flowers that give pollen to the honey you are working with can lend themselves to different magical uses as well.

Acacia—This exotically flavored honey carries a bright, floral smell and is nurturing magic for soothing fear and instilling a gentle warmth.

Alfalfa—Alfalfa has been associated with money magic for millennia because it is such a valuable crop. Keep a small jar of alfalfa honey in the cabinet to keep money in the home.

Avocado—Associated with love, lust, and fertility, the California honey made from avocado flowers has a taste that is sweet and also buttery. Use in magic when self-love or stirring passions are called for.

Blueberry—This airy and lightly flavored honey is the result of the hard work of bees in Michigan and New England. Blueberries are pollinated by heavy buzzers, the bumblebees. However, honey bees can't resist that sweet nectar either. Blueberry honey, as well as the berries themselves, is associated with physical and psychic protection.

Buckwheat—This dark and brooding honey is filled with the feeling of the fields where the bees gather their nectar. It is a robust taste and can overwhelm more delicate flavors if used to excess. Buckwheat is associated with Venus and protection, so it should be used to protect loved ones as well as yourself. Those Venusian associations can also be used to guard your finances, where all the beauty and artful associations ring true.

Clover—One of the most popularly available commercial kinds of honey, red clover lends a round, floral taste, while white clover has a bright, high note to its mild flavor. Clover is associated with good luck, so add it when a little boost is needed, as it can help win over the opposition and add strength to your case.

Eucalyptus—Eucalyptus adds an intense flavor to this honey from California. There are over 420 cultivated species of the eucalyptus tree. The magic of eucalyptus is in grounding harmful energies and breaking hexes, as well as inspiring focused thought and discernment. The scent is refreshing and can be mildly medicinal-smelling.

Lavender—The mellow nature of lavender lends itself to peaceful and harmonizing workings, and can be added to teas when getting to the root of a problem is of the utmost importance. It helps to uncover secrets. This sought-after honey is produced from Northern California to Washington State. It pairs well with mint.

Orange blossom—This immensely popular honey, produced in California, Texas, and Florida, features delicate citrus flavors derived from the variety of citrus groves in the production area. Bitter orange, sweet orange varieties, lemon, grapefruit, and lime are often grown nearby, lending flavors of all of the above to the resulting honey. Citruses have solar associations and, as such, can be used for the magic of abundance, protection, acceptance, creativity, banishing depression, balance, and prosperity.

Sage—This plant is invoked for magic concerning intelligence, wisdom, and rational thought as well as protection magic and wish-granting. The resulting honey can provide introspection when added to teas while mulling over a problem. This California native honey is frequently blended into other honey to preserve its flow.

Thyme—Bring the magic of purification with this honey, produced all over the United States. Thyme magic is an intuitive connection, psychic development and growth, as well as clairvoyance. The hardy nature and woody stem give this small plant a backbone. It instills strength, compassion, and courage.

Tupelo—This Floridian honey is for magic dealing with endurance, stamina, and staying true to yourself.

A word on mead: This wine is made from honey instead of grapes and is one of the oldest beverages around. Don't let the descriptor fool you. Just because this gorgeous wine is made from the distinctly flavored honeys available the world over doesn't mean all mead is sweet. Just as with traditional grape wines, they can have dry, semisweet, and sweet varieties. Look to this list to find the magical associations of the beverage itself. If it is a traditional mead, look for clover honey or orange blossom honey as they are commonly used in meads for their availability, cost, and flavor.

MAGICAL TEA RECIPES

Amounts aren't given for this section, so you can more easily scale it to your needs, palette, and time. Blend a cup at a time, or make larger batches to have on hand for when the time is right.

Business-Boosting Tea for Small-Business Owners

- » Black tea (sense of adventure, bravery)

- » Nutmeg—powdered is fine, but grinding your own is magical; don't use a coffee grinder on nutmeg, or you'll kill the grinder; yes, it's that hard (calming, dreaming, good luck, bringing awareness, creativity, hex breaking, health, justice, focus)

- » Cloves (dispelling negativity, hex breaking, mental powers, prosperity, protection, purification)

- » Star anise (protection, purification, growth)

Place tea in infusion equipment (tea ball, filter, infuser, or bag). Add aromatics before pouring the water. Crush the star anise with the flat side of a chef's knife to release the full flavor. Make sure to use a tight-fitting lid after pouring the hot water. Otherwise, all of the volatile oils are escaping on the breeze, and reducing the amount of gorgeous flavor this tea will have. As you grind your herbs and wait for the tea to steep (5 minutes), envision all of the bright new faces who will find your business. These aren't just any customers, they are your dream customers. Remember, a rising tide lifts all ships. The people who are supposed to find your work, will.

Seize the Day! Tea

» Maté tea—from the holly family, more caffeine than coffee, beware! (healing, focus, courage, drive)

» Ginger (to speed the magic, energizing, passion, power, courage)

» Cayenne (to speed the magic, protection, prosperity)

» Allspice (beating the competition, achievement)

Peppers make sweet things taste sweet, so the heat of the tea can be tempered with lemon, or sugar and cream, depending on your palette. Drink this one in the morning and you will be ready to sack Rome by the time you make it to work.

My Lover's Arms Tea

» Honeybush tea base (comforting, caffeine-free)

» Dried peaches (love, peace, acceptance)

» Vanilla (calm, clarity, love, passion)

» Optional: apricot (creativity, defense against evil, knowledge of goodness in the world, optimism, passion, love, banishing distrust)

Need the comfort of a lover's embrace? Blend this tea for the loving strength and support you are looking for.

"Talk to Me, Bob" Tea

» Rooibos tea (grounded strength)

» Blanched almonds (beauty, money, peace, fortune, hope, rebirth, communication, business desires)

» Peppermint (clarity, happiness, healing, acquiring material objects, purification)

This blend of herbs is designed to open the lines of communication and keep them open.

Serenity of the Moon Tea

Prepare a jasmine green tea with lemon juice or three white grapes, halved and added to the tea after sugar if desired. They will cool the tea and add a hint of sweetness. It does what it says, bringing the peace you (and I) feel when looking up to the moon at night, during full moon rituals, and when in community with our true fellows.

Solar Flare Protection Tea

» Black tea (courage)

» Rosemary—double the amount of herb if using fresh instead of dried (strength)

» Orange peel (protection)

Rosemary is one of my favorite herbs to use as a sweet as well as a savory; we tend to think of our green herbs as savory only, but one sip of my rosemary steamer, and you'll be singing another tune.

There are two preparation methods. The first is to make an orange pekoe tea and flavor it with rosemary syrup (check the section on infused spirits in Chapter 8 for my rosemary syrup recipe).

The second is to blend a full-leaf black tea, then add blood orange peel and fresh rosemary. Bonus points if you heat the water with the rosemary in it to release its full flavor.

Mixing Drinks
and Friends

When grateful gatherings become selective soirées, knowing what to have on hand, how to prepare it, and how to pair it can make a party perfect. Whether you're having a casual planning session for a large group event, or throwing a huge bash to celebrate your big promotion, getting guests in the mood will guarantee they'll be talking about it for a long time.

HOW TO DESIGN THE PERFECT
SIGNATURE DRINK

When enjoying the presence of friends, or magical practitioners, the ability to craft a delightful cocktail is a rare treat. Anyone can follow a recipe and make the same old, tired margarita. Instead of falling back on an old, reliable cocktail, why not create something they have never seen before, and really knock their socks off?

What's the occasion?

Having the type of gathering in mind will help develop the correct feeling for your drink before you put out the wrong glassware or stumble over garnishes. Your cocktail should reflect a) who you are, b) the mood of the event (if not the theme), and c) the attendees. If you're looking to gather your fellow law professors for a quiet night of court-house gossip and cheese, your drink will have a different mood from a post-holiday retail store "Holy cow we survived the holidays" party, or an adult slumber party for your coven mates. If you're having a staid gathering, think original takes on classic cocktails. Raucous gatherings of closer friends allow for more adventurous drinks, and an intimate gatherings of very close confidantes makes room for something that shows your personality, while making memories that are likely to turn into an in-joke later. While "Renatta's Sidecar," "Sally's Jumble Fizz," and "Larry's Latenight Luxury Cocktail" all have different feelings, it's up to a good host or hostess to know how to read the crowd. An irrever-ent cocktail selection can encourage chatter and enliven conversation, while a new take on a classic will let people know that you have sophisti-cated tastes but still enjoy trying new things. Another side of that would be making a signature cocktail for a funeral or wake. You wouldn't want something overly cheery or childish.

How much do you know about cocktails?

An honest assessment of your abilities is a must for this exercise. If you have a passing familiarity with spirits because you watch TV shows about drinking, you might try something less tricky to make but that still says you made an effort. For this I'd suggest a cocktail based on a shrub from Chapter 8. Something like a watermelon and prosecco vinegar shrub would pair well with a botanical gin, rather than a tradi-tional one. A popular rose and cucumber gin sounds like just the ticket for a summer afternoon gathering on the patio. Vinegar-based shrubs are cooling on the body, so they will relax people in the heat and allow them to enjoy the flavors of the season. It is easy to master, and by mak-ing your own syrup to flavor the cocktails, you keep the price down and inspire people to think you're a bartending legend they knew nothing about.

What time of year is it?

Making sure your cocktail is seasonally appropriate is an important step, because you don't want to jar the guests out of their party mood. I wouldn't serve a hot tea cocktail in summer, and the same goes for a frozen drink in a blizzard.

As a good host, consider if your cocktail could have a mocktail counterpart for attendees who aren't drinking.

Asking "leaded or unleaded" or some such variation allows guests to pick how they would like to moderate their alcohol intake without making a big deal out of it. Remember, no one owes anyone else an explanation as to why they don't drink; it could be a myriad of reasons, but it's really no one's business. By the same token, whether you're doing invitations, an electronic invite, or word of mouth, letting people know there will be mocktails and alcohol alternatives will help people, who otherwise might have skipped for fear of limited drink options, feel welcomed.

Think of the drink's parts as categories, rather than singular ingredients.

That will put you on your way to making a delicious drink with your own flair. Sarah Mitchell, manager of London's Lab Bar, said in a 2008 interview with *The Guardian*, before you go mixing bottles of expensive liquor trying to find just the right balance, make lemonade. The idea is that you will have to find just the right balance of water, sugar, and lemon. It'll teach you to have a gentle hand with sours like lemon, while feeling out the right balance of all three. Learning that balance is just like making a shrub cocktail: one part syrup, one part alcohol, four parts sparkling water. Stir gently. (Recipes are given in parts to allow for scaling purposes. You can make one glass by turning those parts into ounces, or make a pitcher by turning them into cups.)

Practice, practice, practice!

Once you have an idea of what you would like to create, allow yourself room for errors and time to perfect the drink. Have a bestie come over the day before and try out variations on the theme, and see which one they like best. In the case of the shrub-based drinks, they're already sober friendly; just add an additional part of sparkling water where the alcohol would be. A good ratio is 1:1:2—one part sweetness, one part tartness, two parts alcohol. The last two parts can be made of two different alcohols, but try to keep them along the same lines, so they don't clash on the palate. Adding triple sec to a margarita gives it a little jazz because the orange flavor is still within the realm of citrus. A rusty nail is a classic because Drambuie liquor is still a whiskey at heart.

Oleosaccharum—"oil sugar"—discussed in depth at the end of Chapter 8, is a great base for a punch (with or without booze) and scales down easily for individual servings. This is a delicious, citrusy, brightening syrup that extracts all of the precious oil from the peel of the fruit, without losing much of it to the air. ½ part oleosaccharum, 1 part alcohol, 4 parts sparkling water, garnish. Stir gently.

Be willing to accept feedback.

Not every drink will entice every person, but if you're getting a lot of feedback, look at what you're accomplishing and how.

CREATING SEASONAL COCKTAILS FOR GROUP RITUALS, PARTIES, AND MORE

1. Grab a notepad and a pen and sit where you won't be disturbed.

2. Take four sheets of paper and fold them in half top to bottom. Label each half for the eight sabbats of the witch's year: *Samhain, Yule, Imbolc, Ostara, Beltane, Litha, Lughnasadh, Mabon*. (If you celebrate other holy tides, adjust accordingly.)

3. Under each holy tide, list the flavors, colors, and feelings associated with each festival.

4. Look at the colors, flavors, and feelings that are embodied in each celebration. Look toward the feelings and colors to give context clues on how the drink should be prepared. If the feeling is cozy, you might choose a warm cocktail like a toddy.

By working out your thoughts on paper before you start to play alchemist, you will save time and money on your hobby. It also gives you a chance to plan ahead if you are going to incorporate cordials, ingredients, or syrups that need to be prepared ahead of time.

What to Do with Leftover Potions

With all of these incredible options, what do you do with leftover potions?

"Leftover wine, what's that?" jokes Aunt Pat. While it might not be a common occurrence to have wine that needs a home, this chapter is filled with ideas to extend the life and usefulness of your magical brews.

LIBATION!

While current vernacular might have you thinking that drinking any alcoholic beverage would be synonymous with libation, the word actually refers to wine and drinks poured in honor of a deity. So whether it is apple juice with coven mates or mead with a friend, leftover drinks can be poured out in praise of a favorite deity. Each deity will have their favorites, of course; think of the height of their worship and you'll find your way to their preferred drinks. I buy the Irish goddess known as the Morrigan 18- to 21-year-old single malt scotch. Deities of the African diaspora are associated with rum. Once, I reached for the devotional bottle of rum and a certain entity indicated he'd rather have the absinthe in the other cabinet. It wasn't until later that my brain caught up with the rest of me. "Oh!" I remembered how popular absinthe was among the French and Creole adherents. It made perfect sense. So if you have a gut feeling, follow that trail to its logical end.

SWEETS

Crème Fraîche and Lavender Black Pepper Cheesecake

Tools

» 8" round springform pan

» Parchment paper

» Mixer with paddle attachment, or a rubber scraper

» Wax paper or plastic wrap

Ingredients

» Unsalted butter (nurturing, fertility, prosperity)

» 1½ cups heavy cream (nurturing, fertility, prosperity)

» 1 tsp. ground lavender pepper—see Constant Conversation Lavender Pepper Grinder recipe on page 216

» 12 oz. cream cheese—room temperature (nurturing, fertility, prosperity)

» ¾ cup crème fraîche, whole milk yogurt, or sour cream (nurturing, fertility, prosperity)

» ⅓ cup sugar (love, lust, fertility)

» 2 large eggs—room temperature (prosperity)

» 2 tbsp. lemon juice (increasing the power of a spell)

» 1 vanilla bean (passion, calm, relaxation)

Constant Conversation Lavender Pepper Grinder

Tools

» Pepper mill

Ingredients

» Leftover lavender

» Peppercorns

If you have lavender left over from lemonade, syrup making, or other baking adventure, it's time to experiment with it as a savory spice. This flower acts more like a seed and its almost minty and camphor-like aroma makes it a great ally of savory dishes. Instead of plain ground black pepper, try making your own pepper mill filled with layers of peppercorns interspersed with lavender flowers. It adds a depth to the pepper that is otherwise not found in culinary adventures. Don't worry, it won't taste like your grandma's fancy bathroom soap. But it does make for a great conversation over dinner. Black pepper is energizing and lavender helps divulge secrets, so no more one-word answers to "How was your day?" around the dinner table. Enliven the conversations with a hand from our botanical allies.

Preheat the oven to 350°F.

Butter the springform pan. Place a round of parchment in the bottom of the pan and butter the paper as well.

Find the paddle attachment for the mixer and beat the cream cheese and sugar on medium speed for about 3 minutes. It should be smooth at this point.

You don't want too much air in the mix so if you don't have a paddle attachment, use a rubber scraper to fold the ingredients together.

Cut the vanilla bean down the middle lengthwise and scrape out the seeds. Add the seeds and the lavender pepper to the cream cheese mixture. You can add the vanilla seedpod to your sugar bowl for a lightly vanilla-flavored sugar.

Beat in sour cream and lemon juice. Add eggs one at a time, mixing between eggs. Remember to scrape down the bowl for full integration. Mix in cream until incorporated.

Pour cheese batter into prepared springform pan. Place the springform into a large roasting pan. Fill the roaster with hot water to a depth of 1 inch. Bake until the edges are fully set and the center wiggles slightly when shaken, 75–90 minutes. Remove the roasting pan from the oven and place the springform pan on a wire baking rack to cool.

Feel free to sprinkle some powdered cloves in the hot roasting pan water and set it back in the oven with the door cracked. It'll add clove fragrance to the air, and cloves bring luck into the home.

Once the cheesecake is cool to the touch, cover in wax paper or plastic wrap and place in the refrigerator for a minimum of 3 hours, ideally overnight. To unmold, run a knife or spatula around the inside edge of the pan, invert onto another plate, and peel off the parchment, or open the springform and remove. Optional: garnish with whipped cream (fertility) and a pinch of lavender flowers (healing).

Lollipops

During the early days of my tea shop, I was looking for new and exciting ways to use the magical teas I had blended and came upon a recipe for homemade lollipops. All we are really doing is replacing water with a strong tea made with intention, and voilà! Magical lollipops. Lollipops disappear naturally, so why not use that to your advantage?

Tools

Make sure all of this is assembled before starting. Candy making moves fast!

» Good weather—humid/rainy days can make it hard for the candy to set

» Saucepan

» Candy thermometer—available in kitchen and craft stores

» Silicone pastry brush

» Silicone baking mats or lollipop molds

» Lollipop sticks—or make candies instead

» Paper towels—candy making is messy business

Ingredients

» 1 cup sugar (love, joy, lust)

» ½ cup light corn syrup (fertility, agreement, balance)

» ¼ cup strong tea—magical teas can be used here; think citrus flavors for prosperity, protection, and purification, or see Chapter 8 for magical applications of fruits

» Nonflavored cooking spray—to keep the candy from sticking to mold

» Optional: 1½ tsp. commercial flavorings

» Optional: food coloring

Prepare your magical space. Coat the inside of the mold with a small amount of cooking oil then wipe away the excess. This should leave a light film of oil on the mold without making the candy oily. Place sticks in the molds if using them. Consider ringing a small bell to raise the vibration of your work space.

Add corn syrup, sugar, and tea water to a medium-sized saucepan over medium heat.

Stir consistently until the sugar is incorporated. (Stir clockwise to bring in a desire, like money. Stir counterclockwise to banish something, like fear.) Once it's boiling, check the temperature (candy thermometers with a clip-on attachment can help make sure you don't get burned during this stage). You want the mixture to reach the hard crack stage, or 300°F (around 150°C).

Remove the saucepan from heat and place on a heatproof surface like a trivet. Allow it to cool until the mixture is no longer bubbling. Stir in food coloring and flavor at that point, if desired.

Gently pour sugar mixture into molds, making sure to completely cover the top of the stick, so they can be enjoyed easily. If making candies instead, keep stirring for a few more moments, allowing the gel to cool a few more degrees before pouring. It will be stickier, but will hold shape better the colder it is, if using a silicone baking mat.

Allow the candies to cool completely before handling. Wrap, and decorate if desired. Using colors corresponding to holytides is a seasonal treat.

Love and Romance Whiskey Bread Pudding

Tools

- » Mixing bowl (medium)
- » Baking dish

Ingredients

- » 1 lb. bread, cubed (prosperity, blessings of divine)
- » 6 eggs, beaten (fertility, prosperity)
- » 4 cups milk (nurturing, fertility, prosperity)
- » 1½ cups sugar (lust, love)
- » 1 cup heavy cream (nurturing, fertility, prosperity)
- » ½ cup golden raisins (banishing sorrow, fertility, accomplishments)
- » 1 tbsp. vanilla extract—see page 163 (mental powers, passion, relaxing)
- » ½ tbsp. cinnamon (good luck, creativity, protection)

Sauce

Tools

» Saucepan

» Whisk

Ingredients

» 1 ½ cups sugar (lust, love)

» ¾ cup butter (nurturing, fertility, prosperity)

» ¾ cup corn syrup (fertility, releasing subconscious tension, agreement)

» ½ cup whiskey (sex, offerings, marriage, healing)

While the bread pudding bakes, make the sauce. In a saucepan, place corn syrup, sugar, and butter and stir over low heat. When thoroughly blended, remove from heat and whisk in whiskey. Serve warm over bread pudding.

Preheat oven to 300°F (165°C)

Add sugar to a medium mixing bowl, and whip eggs into the bowl. Stir in cinnamon, vanilla extract, milk, and heavy cream. Stir until incorporated.

Place bread cubes in a buttered baking dish. Sprinkle raisins on top of bread and pour cream mixture over bread. Allow it to soak for 5 minutes before placing in the oven. Cook for 45 minutes, or until golden brown. Serve warm with sauce.

Preserved Lemons

If you've been around in the spring for limoncello (or lime-oncello) you know that it's easy to have a few fruits hanging around without another thing to infuse. When that happens, it's time to make preserved lemons!

Tools

» Small bowl

» Quart-sized mason jar, sterilized

Ingredients

» 3 lemons (calming, purification of disease, energizing, honesty)

» ½ cup sugar (sweetness)

» ½ cup kosher salt (purification)

Cut the lemons into slices.

Mix salt and sugar in a small bowl and put it off to the side.

Place a lemon slice in the bottom of the jar, and sprinkle salt sugar mixture over it. Alternate lemon slices and salt/sugar mixture until the jar is full.

Let sit on the counter for 3 days.

Cap and place in the refrigerator for up to 2 months.

Use the slices whole, or add the rind to compound butters for a lemon butter that can't be beaten. Add preserved lemons to vinaigrette, top salads with olives and cucumbers, make lemon bars, or add it to mayo sauce for fish, bistro chicken, and so many more things. It also makes a zesty and delightful sauce for ravioli with sour cream.

Refrigerator Mini Margarita Cheesecakes

Tools

» Mixing bowl

» Mixer

» Metal tray

» Cupcake papers

Ingredients

- » 8 oz. pkg. cream cheese (fertility, prosperity)

- » 14 oz. sweetened condensed milk (fertility, prosperity)

- » 1 cup whipped dessert topping (some are better than others depending on the oil they're made from; if you have the time to whip cream, do it)

- » 6 oz. can frozen limeade concentrate, thawed (antidepressant, strength, stimulation)

- » ⅓ cup tequila and a splash of triple sec (love, lust, fidelity, protection)

- » Optional: a few drops green food coloring (prosperity, fertility)

- » Optional: Nilla Wafer™ or other vanilla cookie

Take cream cheese out of the refrigerator 10 minutes before beginning, as it will be easier to work with.

Beat cheese until fluffy.

Slowly incorporate condensed milk and limeade concentrate while stirring until smooth.

Add tequila and triple sec, and stir thoroughly.

If desired, add food coloring.

Gently fold in whipped cream or topping.

Refrigerate for 1 hour until semi-firm.

Place cupcake wrappers on a metal tray that will fit in the refrigerator.

Line each wrapper with a cookie; one cookie per wrapper.

Pour margarita mixture over cookies until ⅓ full. Repeat with remaining mixture.

Refrigerate for another hour, minimum. Serve.

Alternatively, try substituting strawberry daiquiri mix and rum.

MEATS

Cocoa-Rubbed Pork Tenderloin

Tools

- » Large skillet or saucepan
- » Aluminum foil
- » Sifter (optional)
- » Small saucepan
- » Meat thermometer

Ingredients

- » 2 lbs. pork tenderloin (prosperity)
- » Unsweetened cocoa powder (loving connection)
- » 3 cups apple cider (Venus, love, beauty, arts, physical action, healing, birth)
- » 3 tbsp. real maple syrup (adding sweetness, to the dish and your life)
- » 2 tbsp. apple cider vinegar (clears away emotional debris)

Preheat a large skillet or saucepan over medium heat, with a bit of oil to prevent sticking. Preheat the oven to 425°F.

Grab a large piece of aluminum foil and lay it on your work surface. Place the tenderloin on top of the foil.

Sprinkle dry cocoa powder all over the tenderloin, turn it over, and repeat. (I use a sifter, but that's optional.) Rub the cocoa into the surface. Place into skillet and allow to sear. (If the cocoa is dry, the rub may burn in the skillet; that's okay, you haven't burned the roast.)

While that is cooking, pour the apple cider, vinegar, and syrup into a small saucepan. Over medium heat, allow to reduce by one third.

The apple cider vinegar will tenderize the pork, while the cider adds sweetness and tang.

After 4 minutes, flip the roast over, and continue searing on the other side.

When 8 minutes have passed, place the roast into a roasting pan, and pour the apple cider reduction over the roast. (At this stage you can add potatoes and carrots if desired.)

Place into the oven and roast for another 20 minutes or until the meat thermometer reaches 145°.

Allow the roast to rest for 5–10 minutes before slicing. Use the pan sauce as a delightful gravy, and enjoy!

Tea-Brined Pork Tenderloin

Black tea has an active flavor profile for marinating pork. I was working some banishing magic in my life and wanted to bring the best intentions when creating this meal. I brewed a strong black tea with whole black peppercorns for a sweet, warm aroma.

Tools

- » Roasting pan
- » Whisk
- » Aluminum foil
- » Meat thermometer

Ingredients

- » A good-sized tenderloin for the number of dinner guests—a good rule is to buy 8 oz. per person (prosperity)
- » 2 cups black tea—brew it at double strength with peppercorns (protection, sex magic, strength)

» 2 tbsp. black peppercorns (mental alertness, physical strength, courage, banishing, uncrossing, driving away evil)

» 2 tbsp. flour (abundance, spirits, blessings, wealth, harvest, luck)

Preheat the oven to 425°F.

After marinating the tenderloin in the refrigerator for a day, pour the marinade into the roasting pan. Next, whisk in the flour to thicken the mix as it cooks. Place the tenderloin in the center of the pan, add cracked black pepper and salt to the top of the roast, and cover with foil.

Roast in the oven for 20 minutes. Then remove foil, whisk gravy to avoid lumps, and lower oven temperature to 400°. Roast for another 10–15 minutes until the meat thermometer reads 145° internal temperature.

Once cooked thoroughly, remove from pan and allow to rest on cutting board for 10 minutes. Slice and serve.

I may have used this recipe for banishing work, but black pepper is associated with uncrossing, courage, driving away evil, physical energy, and mental alertness.

Turkey Breast Poached in Ginger Ale

The spicy ginger ale that I get from the specialty grocery store, whoa. It'll clear your sinuses. Ask me how I know. It may have also made my eyes water. My sinuses are nowhere to be found. Now I make my own ginger ale by making a ginger syrup and adding it to sparkling water (see page 184 for recipe). Instead of letting this magical powerhouse go to waste, I poached a turkey breast in it.

When I say ginger is a powerhouse, I mean it raises energy and adds a powerful boost to magical workings. Ginger can be used for astral projection (and having a belly full of turkey can help anyone nap out), and the fire of ginger adds love, passion, and beauty to a working. Ginger is useful for money spells, protection potions, and purification as well.

Tools

» Dutch oven

» Small bowl

» meat thermometer

Ingredients

» 2 lbs. turkey breasts (comfort, nurturing, blessing)

» 4 cups ginger ale (luck, healing, prosperity, lust)

» 1 onion, quartered (banishing, hex breaking)

» 2 stalks celery, chopped (concentration, lust, banishing enemies, sleep)

» 1 ginger thumb, peeled and sliced into coins (luck, love, money, purification)

» 2 tsp. flour (binding everything together, abundance, advice, harvest, growth)

» 1 tbsp. butter (nurturing, protection, prosperity)

» 1 bay leaf (attraction, exorcism, good luck, harmony)

Place the Dutch oven on stovetop and turn heat to medium. Add a tablespoon of oil to the pot as it warms. Take ¼ of the onion and separate it into layers. Sprinkle the onion's segments in the bottom of the pan to caramelize, stirring frequently.

Once the onion is carmelized, lay the turkey breast on the bottom of the pan.

Place the rest of the onion, celery, ginger, and bay leaf into the pot and pour ginger ale over them. Place the lid on and bring to a boil.

After it comes to a boil, lower the temperature and simmer for 20 minutes or until the meat thermometer reads 165°F.

While that simmers, grab a small bowl and put the flour into it. Then add a tablespoon of cold water at a time to the flour, mixing with a fork to create a slurry.

Remove breasts from the pot once they are fully cooked and remove solids to the bin. To make gravy, add the flour slurry to the stock in the pan and mix well. Leave it on medium heat, stirring frequently.

Once the gravy thickens, add a tablespoon of butter and allow it to melt and incorporate. Pour over chicken, noodles, rice, potatoes—whatever.

OTHER TREATS

Beer Bread

While beer has fallen out of favor as a ritual libation, it is easy to have some on hand after a gathering. Each different style of beer will have its own unique taste, and that makes for a great variety in the kitchen.

Tools

- » Mixing bowl (large)
- » Sifter
- » Loaf pan
- » Wire rack

Ingredients

- » 3 cups self-rising flour (wealth, luck, prosperity)
- » 12 oz. beer—any style, flavor, or profile (love, fertility, sexual potency, healing, marriage)
- » 3 tbsp. sugar (blessings, love, sex, fertility, prosperity)
- » Optional: pinch of salt (purification)
- » Melted butter for top of loaf

Preheat oven to 350°F (or 165°C)

Sift flour and sugar (and salt if desired) together to add a lighter texture.

Add beer to flour/sugar mixture and stir quickly so that all of the flour is incorporated before the beer soaks in. Once thoroughly combined, let rest in mixing bowl. Grab your loaf pan and grease it with oil or butter to keep the bread from sticking.

Pour dough into greased loaf pan. Bake for 55–60 minutes, until the top of the loaf is golden brown. In the last 10 minutes of baking, top with butter if desired. Cool on wire rack.

Chai Deviled Eggs

While blending my Fiery Wall of Protection chai (chai means tea, so chai tea is redundant) I wanted ways to incorporate the flavors of the peppercorns, cloves, and other spices into my cooking. The longer these woody spices are exposed to heat and water, the stronger they become. I boiled my eggs in strong chai to make deviled eggs so that the spice could permeate the egg whites, rather than merely flavoring the yolk mixture. At Ostara eggs are plentiful, and this is a great way to use them up.

Traditional chai uses spices like:

»   Cloves (hex breaking, prosperity, purification)

»   Cardamom (confidence, courage, purpose)

»   Ginger (love, passion, courage, hex breaking, luck)

»   Cinnamon (creativity, mood-lifting, protection)

Tools

»   Egg piercer

»   Saucepan

»   Slotted spoon

»   Large bowl of ice

» Sharp knife

» Bowl for yolks

Ingredients

» Strong chai

» 12 eggs—hint: eggs that are a few days older are more comfortable to peel (fertility)

» 1 tbsp. Dijon mustard (memory, awareness, strength, courage)

» ⅓ cup mayonnaise—don't even think of using Miracle Whip (fertility, wishes granted, prosperity)

» 1 tbsp. minced shallot (protection, healing, strength)

» 1tsp. hot sauce (banishing, purification, protection)

» Salt, pepper, and smoked paprika to taste (purification, banishing, prosperity)

I prefer to steam my eggs, rather than boil them, but for the flavor of the chai, we will boil them. I puncture the bottom of the eggshells with a punch designed for that to make them easier to peel and allow the chai inside the shell.

Place the eggs into the saucepan and add enough cold, strong chai to cover the eggs by an inch. If you don't have enough tea, add water and a few peppercorns and cloves.

Place the lid on the saucepan and turn the heat on to high. Then bring the liquid to a rolling boil. Boil the eggs for 8 minutes for a firm yolk.

Using a slotted spoon, transfer each egg to an ice bath, to stop the cooking process and make the eggs easier to peel. Note: the eggs can be stored for up to one week at this unpeeled stage.

Peel the eggs. I like to use a large bowl and swirl the eggs around, bumping them into each other in the cold water to loosen the shells for peeling. After peeling use a sharp knife to cut each egg in half lengthwise. Place the yolk into a bowl, and the egg white halves on a serving tray.

When all the eggs have been peeled, cut, and separated, it is time to make the filling. Taking a fork, mash each yolk into a crumbling powder. To the bowl of cooked yolks, add the mayo, Dijon mustard, shallot, and hot sauce. Give the mixture a good stir before adding salt, pepper, and paprika.

Scoop the yolk mixture into a pastry bag with a preferred tip, or simply place a plastic bag in a tall glass, fold over the opening, and scoop the mixture into the container. Cut the tip off the plastic bag to make a small opening for the yolks to be dispensed.

Fill each egg half with mixture, and top with cracked black pepper to complement the spices in the chai.

Shrub Glaze for Meats and Veggies

In the chapter Fruit Feeling Frisky, we talked about the glory of a shrub or drinking vinegar. This blend of fruit, vinegar, and sugar makes an incredible base for glazes, as the combinations are infinite. Making fish? Consider something light and crisp like the watermelon and Prosecco vinegar shrub or a cucumber cider vinegar shrub. A mushroom cap grilled over an open flame? Try a plum balsamic shrub.

Tools

- » Sauté pan

Ingredients

- » ½ cup of the shrub of choice—the fruit provides sugar and the vinegar provides flavor and breaks the cell walls of food for easier digestion
- » ⅓ cup stock or 1 stock concentrate packet

» Additional aromatics for flavor—onion, shallot, scallions, rosemary, garlic, ginger, and the like

Sauté chopped aromatics in oil to release flavor. Add shrub and stock to the hot pan. Reduce heat and stir until thickened. Consider adding honey or jam as a thickener. The glaze is ready when it sticks to the back of the spoon. Pour over desired foods.

Bonus: Try sautéed fruits and glaze made with tea or water for a zingy dessert! Peaches with ginger glaze and lavender garnish is a particularly lovely treat. This simple trick will have your friends and family thinking you're a gourmet chef!

Tea-Smoked Foods

This traditional Chinese cooking style is great for adding a smoky flavor to chicken, fish, seafood, tofu, and even mushrooms!

Tools

» Aluminum foil (a few layers thick)

» Wok

» Steamer basket or wire rack

» Lid or additional foil

Ingredients

» Blended tea leaves (with or without magical intent)—you can use Lapsang souchong to up the smoky flavor, jasmine green tea for a subtle floral note that is great with seafood, while some dried citrus rind will impart a tangy taste to the smoke for chicken

» Dry white rice (uncooked)

Place the wok on the cooking surface and cover the cooking area with several layers of aluminum foil.

Take the amount of tea you have prepared, and add the same amount of white rice for a 1:1 ratio of tea leaves to rice. This will make sure the smoke isn't too loud or harsh. Add the tea and rice mixture to the wok and turn on the heat to medium.

When the mixture begins to smoke, add the food to be cooked to the steamer basket and cover. Allow the heat and smoke to cook the food until ready.

A Cautious Witch: Things to Consider

When working as magical practitioners, we must always act with intent, attention, and forethought. That goes doubly for witches who create potions, elixirs, and other beneficial ephemera. We cannot blame a devil we don't believe in if something goes wrong, even more so if you got what you asked for, but still aren't happy.

A WORD OF CAUTION, OR A FEW THOUSAND OF THEM

We must always take care that the ingredients we use, the preparation of our space, and the materials we create are of the best quality possible, in the best environment possible. This doesn't mean, however, that you need a movie-sized budget and can only source materials under the full moon in Virgo during a solar eclipse. Remember, you are the magic. Having nifty robes and exotic wooden wands is lovely, but it's all just stuff. You only really need three things for magic, "me, myself, and I," or more seriously:

» Connection
» Intention

» Sending Energy

Magic is the summation of your drive to accomplish a goal.

Step 1: Connection

Grounding and centering, or creating a connection, doesn't mean to goddesses, gods, Spirit, or the Universe. Though it can, it should be to the earth itself. The purpose of centering and connection in magic is to remind ourselves of the world outside and to use that connection to provide a generative force for your magical application. That generative force can be accomplished through dance, song, chanting, or doing the Hokey Pokey. Raising energy provides fuel for your Step 2: Intention.

Raising energy, whether through connecting to the earth and sending its energy out, or raising energy and directing it, ensures that you are not depleting your own personal power. This common mistake is easy to diagnose. After connecting to the earth, raising energy, then sending it to the universe, you should feel energized, awake, and renewed. If you feel sluggish, tired, or like you just walked ten miles through mud, the issue is with the centering connection. In that case, practice grounding techniques and meditation.

Step 2: Intention

Intention comes after connection because you need to decide on the outcome before the magic begins. Your spell starts the moment you choose to act. Whether your spell is a stated need or an untenable situation, the spell is sparked in your mind in some way. The intention, when actively working the spell, is the definitive statement within the active spell working that seals the action. If your choice is money, then your intention could be "I have the money I need to pay this parking ticket." The intention is clearly stated, positively worded, and direct. We talked about wording spells in the positive instead of the negative in Chapter 2 because psychology teaches us that our subconscious doesn't understand things worded in the negative. So if you start from "I have enough money to pay my parking ticket," you are already visualizing the space where prosperity will land, and the effortless nature of the blessing.

Step 3: Sending Energy

The essential part of all of this is the sending of energy. Anyone can raise energy—I've been to churches as a teen that raised enough power to make the hair on your arms stand up—but if nothing is directing the power, it doesn't matter how much gets raised. It sort of lingers around in the space for a while and slowly dissipates over time. Those practiced in the art of feeling the energy can step into a place of power and know it, whether it be temple, church, garden, or grove.

This sending of energy is why some traditions place such a high importance on circle casting. For the newer practitioners among us, circles are cast as a boundary. Whether that circle is cast to keep energy inside or to protect those inside from entities outside depends on the magic, tradition, and ritual taking place. In group work (not everyone who works in a group belongs to a coven; occasionally groups of solitary practitioners gather for magical workings for celebration, needed change, and more), the boundary of the circle keeps the energy moving towards the group goal until being released by the high priestess. This is sometimes referred to as the Cone of Power.

In much solitary work, circle casting has gone out of favor, as many witches don't feel the effort is worth it. They're both right. For some workings, casting a circle is not needed. If you are lighting a candle for a quick blessing before a trying day at work? No need to cast a circle. However, if your best friend is going through testing for cancer and asks for a healing spell, or blessing, do the circle casting. Why? 1) It is easier to build the energy and send it all at once for a larger working. Think of it like popping a balloon You've just spent time stretching it, blowing it up, tying the knot. You're letting all the air out at once, rather than placing a small hole in it for the magic to leak out over time. 2) Magic is about intention, yours as the person casting the spell, but also that of your friend who is receiving the healing work.

It's up to you to know your friend. If you think she'd be better served by having her anoint a candle and light it while you both talk over a cup of tea, great. But if she's really scared, not just nervous, the circle casting serves two purposes: funneling that energy at the right time, and ritual theater. Do not underestimate the importance of ritual theater. While we know the magic comes from within us, having your friend watch you put on a robe or dress candles, put out the full altar spread, lay some fluffy pillows out for her to lie on, and maybe anoint her with oil (who cares if it's olive oil from the grocery store down the street; she doesn't need to know that), helps *her* belief, her confidence in her prognosis, and her eventual cure.

THE LAW OF CONTAGION

What is that? Keeping a clean work space means ease of use, lack of contamination, and less waste from accidental spills. The most important word in that previous sentence was *contamination*.

Even if we are not working with baneful herbs, our teas, syrups, and even cheesecake can become contaminated by an inattentive witch. If a rose petal falls into Susy's tea while she is blending, without her knowledge, it could be completely harmless. However, if Susy is blending that tea for a sick friend with an allergy to roses, it could easily go from just cringe-worthy to life-threatening.

Does the rose affect the magical intention of the tea Susy is creating? Absolutely. Witches work with something called the Law of Contagion. This law of magic doesn't have the press of the misleading and misunderstood Threefold Law of Return (there's more on that in the intro if you missed it). The Law of Contagion means that I can take a drop of full-moon water and add it to a gallon of water, and now it's a gallon of full-moon water. I can't take the drop of moon water back out of that gallon. The same goes for Susy's tea. While she's chopping and mixing herbs, if she doesn't see the petal fall in and starts grinding the herbs, the rose is in there to stay. A few pieces of petal can be fished out, but a) never all the bits, and b) the petal will never be whole again. While you can fish a pebble out of a glass of water, you can't remove one drop of food coloring from the gallon of water. Filtering would take out the red color, but it will never recreate that drop of food coloring.

This is also beneficial when working with precious materials. One piece of a hard-to-find plant works just as well as a handful and is much more fiscally responsible.

BUT THAT'S POISON!

As a witch with a penchant for growing things, I'm continually daydreaming about lovely flowering plants and researching new ones. So, you can imagine how often I'm approached and asked for floral and landscaping advice. Some people get very intimidated by poisonous flowers and plants. I'll let you in on a little secret: unless it's one of the famous poisons, deadly nightshade, wolf's bane, or something like that, most people don't know a poison plant from a beneficial one.

Many of them cross both boundaries. Cherry bark is used for flavoring; it also is used to treat colds and other illnesses. But the leaves have high levels of a chemical that breaks down in the human body as cyanide. Tomato plants are part of the nightshade family, and their leaves as well as the leaves of potatoes and eggplant are toxic and contain a glycoalkaloid called solanine. Green tomatoes also contain an alkaloid called tomatine. The leaves are poisonous enough that people were so afraid of them, when the plants arrived in the early modern-era Europe (1500s), they were blamed for witchcraft and thought to create werewolves.

Just as with the rest of life, pretty doesn't mean good, and ugly doesn't mean bad. That only works in stories. Poisons have their place. Belladonna juice is synthesized for medically dilating pupils to diagnose diseases of the eye. Its cardiac benefits led to its use in medicines to regulate heartbeat. Its active chemical component, atropine, is used in negligent poisonings and chemical warfare remedies. This brings us to my next point:

NATURAL DOES NOT MEAN SAFE

I'm sure that may initially sound like a given, but I have seen it online and in person, and have had people use "but it's natural" as a justification for a whole host of things. Natural items that include herbal supplements are responsible for sixty-nine thousand poisonings each year in the United States alone. What is the difference between medicine and poison? Dosage. It always reminds me of that Terry Pratchet quote, "All fungi are edible. Some are only edible once." So please, educate yourself. There are so many resources available from folk herbalist courses to field guides. Avail yourself of these tools and don't depend on the person selling it to you to know the difference.

A few years ago, a new store opened in a neighboring state. Because I love any excuse for a road trip and shopping is therapeutic, I grabbed a friend and jumped in my vehicle. The most polite word I can use to sum up this experience is "underwhelming." Aside from problematic behaviors related to the owner's inappropriate touching of clients, he was making tinctures that did not list the Latin names of the plants.

While that might seem like a small error, certain plants in the same botanical genus can have vastly different effects on the body. The *Salvia* genus has 986 species of plants that range from hormone balancing to hallucinogenic. Many of them don't even resemble each other. One can grow up to seven feet tall with three-foot diameter leaves, while ornamental sages like hummingbird sage possess dainty flowers and barely reach eleven inches tall.

In this case, he picked a plant that has beneficial lung properties for asthmatics, can cause vomiting, or has hallucinogenic properties, depending on the species of plant chosen. When I asked about the Latin name of the plant, he didn't know.

"I can go look for you. Was there something you were wondering about?"

"I wondered if it was X," (the variety that causes vomiting and grows wild on the East Coast). He goes down into the basement, counts to ten, and comes back, "Yup!"

So, either he was trying to poison people, or he was ignorant of the plants and should not be making and selling "medicines" to the public. As it turns out, he was a member of some company that drop-shipped bulk herbs to him and he was attempting to move inventory without any real understanding of what he was doing.

Closing Thoughts

When I first started this project, I had so many things I wanted to include, but a book can hold only so much knowledge before the pages burst into flame. I am so blessedly lucky to get to share my years of knowledge, experience, and enjoyment with all of you. The best thing I can tell you is that if you give yourself over to the experience of new things, there is an entire world of magic available in this book. It would take a lifetime to master just one or two of these techniques.

All I want is for you to give yourself over to the experience of crafting your own drinks, whether they include spirits or not. Having a parent who is an alcoholic, it was important for me to provide Sober Substitutions.

The last thing I would ever want is for someone to write off this book as being *just* a cocktail guide. Because while this is a potions book, it is intended as a lifeline and a way to use the everyday objects around us to infuse our daily lives with as much magic as we can wring out of each day. Being alive is magical. Birth, life, and death are each their own magic and mystery. If I can empower one person, show one person that the things we do in our daily lives can bring magic and meaning to an otherwise bleak world, I've done a good job.

As always, I do this work for you.

I had a very profound moment while writing the first draft of *Black-thorn's Botanical Magic*. I was struck by a visceral reaction to the idea that my writing was going to live past me and touch people in ways that really had nothing to do with me. That once a book leaves my hands and goes to my (amazing, incredible) editors, my books are no longer mine. They now belong to you. Each person has their own experiences, thoughts, and feelings about my work, and it really has very little to do with me. This is the mark I want to leave on this world and I thank the Gods every day for you joining me on this journey.

In Her Service,

Amy Blackthorn

Botanical
Classification

Allspice (*Pimenta dioica*)
Angelica (*Angelica archangelica*)
Anise (*Pimpinella anisum)*
Apple (*Malus* var., *Pyrus malus*)
Apricot *(Prunus armeniaca)*
Artichoke (*Cynara cardunculus* var. *scolymus)*
Barley (*Hordeum vulgare*)
Basil (*Ocimum basilicum*)
Bay Laurel *(Laurus nobilis)*
Bergamot (*Citrus bergamia*)
Black Pepper *(Piper nigrum)*
Blackthorn (*Prunus spinosa*)
Burdock (*Arctium lappa*)
Calamus (*Acorus calamus*)
Calendula (Calendula officinalis)
Cardamom *(Elettaria cardamomum)*
Cassia (*Cinnamomum cassia*)
Cayenne Pepper (*Capsicum annuum*)
Cedar (*Thuja occidentalis*)
Chamomile (*Matricaria chamomilla, Chamaemelum nobile*)
Cherry (*Prunus* var., *P. avium*)
Chickweed (*Stellaria media*)

Chocolate (*Theobroma cacao*)

Cinnamon *(Cinnamomum verum)*

Clove (*Syzygium aromaticum*)

Coffee (*Coffea arabica*)

Coriander seed (*Coriandrum sativum*)

Corn (*Zea mays*)

Cranberry (*Vaccinium macrocarpon*)

Dandelion (*Taraxacum officinale*)

Fennel (*Foeniculum vulgare*)

Garlic (*Allium sativum*)

Gentian (*Gentiana lutea*)

Ginger (*Zingiber officinale*)

Grains of Paradise (*Aframomum melegueta*)

Grape (*Vitis vinifera*)

Grapefruit (*Citrus paradisi*)

Habanero (*Capsicum chinense c. habanero*)

Honeybush tea (*Cyclopia intermedia*)

Hops (*Humulus lupulus*)

Horseradish *(Armoracia rusticana)*

Hyssop *(Hyssopus officinalis)*

Juniper *(Juniperus communis, osteosperma)*

Lavender *(Lavandula angustifolia)*

Lemon (*Citrus limon*)

Lemon Balm (*Melissa officinalis*)

Lemongrass (*Cymbopogon citratus*)

Lime (*Citrus* × *latifolia, C.* × *aurantiifolia*)

Mandarin *(Citrus reticulata)*

Marigold, French (*Tagetes patula*)

Marjoram (*Origanum majorana*)

Melissa (*Melissa officinalis*)

Mugwort (*Artemisia vulgaris*)

Myrrh (*Commiphora myrrha*)

Onion *(Allium cepa)*
Orris Root (*Rhizoma iridis*)
Parsley (*Petroselinum crispum*)
Parsnip (*Pastinaca sativa*)
Peach (*Prunus persica*)
Peppermint (*Mentha piperita*)
Pine (*Pinus sylvestris*)
Pineapple (*Ananas comosus*)
Rooibos tea (*Aspalathus linearis*)
Rosemary (*Rosmarinus officinalis*)
Sage (*Salvia officianalis*)
Sandalwood (*Santalum album*)
Spicebush (*Lindera benzoin*)
Star Anise (*Illicuim verum*)
Strawberry (*Fragaria virginiana, F. × ananassa*)
Sugarcane (*Saccharum officinarum*)
Sweet Orange (*Citrus sinensis*)
Tangerine (*Citrus reticulata*)
Tansy (*Tanacetum vulgare*)
Tea (*Camellia sinensis*)
Thyme (*Thymus vulgaris*)
Vanilla *(Vanilla planifolia)*
Watermelon (*Citrullus lanatus*)
Wormwood (*Artemisia absinthium*)
Yerba Mate (*Ilex paraguariensis*)
Ylang-ylang (*Cananga odorata*)

Recipe Index

CHAPTER 11—WHAT TO DO WITH LEFTOVER POTIONS

Bibliography

Blackthorn, Amy. *Blackthorn's Botanical Magic*. Newburyport, MA: Weiser Books, 2018.

Blackthorn, Amy. *Sacred Smoke: Clear Away Negative Energies and Purify Body, Mind, and Spirit*. Newburyport, MA: Weiser Books, 2019.

Christensen, Emma. *True Brews*. New York: Random House USA Inc., 2013.

Cunningham, Scott. *Cunningham's Encyclopedia of Magical Herbs*. 2nd ed. Vol. 1. 9th printing. Woodbury, MN: Llewellyn Publications, 2003.

Cunningham, Scott. *Cunninghams Encyclopedia of Wicca in the Kitchen*. Woodbury, MN: Llewellyn Publications, 2005.

Davis, Holly. *Ferment: A Guide to the Ancient Art of Culturing Foods, from Kombucha to Sourdough*. San Francisco: Chronicle Books, 2019.

Enright, Michael J. *Lady with a Mead Cup: Ritual, Prophecy, and Lordship in the European Warband from La Tène to the Viking Age*. Dublin: Four Courts Press, 2013.

Essential Oils Desk Reference. 3rd ed. Vol. 1. Series 1. Orem, UT: Essential Science Publishing, 2008.

"Egtved Girl," the website of the National Museum of Denmark. *en.natmus.dk*

Fothergill, Mark. "A whole lotta shakin.'" *The Guardian*. Guardian News and Media, December 9, 2008. *www.theguardian.com*

Giesecke, Annette Lucia. *The Mythology of Plants: Botanical Lore from Ancient Greece and Rome*. Los Angeles, CA: J. Paul Getty Museum, 2014.

Hall, Judy. *The Crystal Bible*. Alresford, England: Godsfield, 2009.

Heath, Maya. *Magical Oils by Moonlight*. Franklin Lakes, NJ: New Page Books, 2004.

Hellmich, Mittie. *Ultimate Bar Book: The Comprehensive Guide to Over 1,000 Cocktails*. San Francisco: Chronicle Books, 2010.

Holland, Eileen. *Holland's Grimoire of Magickal Correspondences: A Ritual Handbook*. Franklin Lakes, NJ: New Page Books, 2006.

Illes, Judika. *The Element Encyclopedia of 5000 Spells*. New York: Harper One, 2008.

Jeff. "Wine and Chocolate Pairings . . . with Cheese, of Course." Wisconsin Cheeseman Blog, October 24, 2019. *www.wisconsincheeseman.com.*

Latkiewicz, Matthew, and Carl Wiens. *You Suck at Drinking*. Philadelphia: Running Press, 2015.

Owen, James. "Earliest Known Winery Found in Armenian Cave." *National Geographic*, January 12, 2011. Archived from the original on June 3, 2017. Accessed July 8, 2019.

Parsons, Brad Thomas. *Bitters: A Spirited History of a Classic Cure-All, with Cocktails, Recipes, and Formulas*. Berkeley, CA: Ten Speed Press, 2011.

Pendell, Dale, and Gary Snyder. *Pharmako Poeia: Plant Powers, Poisons, and Herbcraft*. Berkeley, CA: North Atlantic Books, 2010.

Perry, Sara. *The Book of Herbal Teas: A Guide to Gathering, Brewing, and Drinking*. San Francisco: Chronicle Books, 1997.

Prada, Luis. "How to Create Your Own Signature Cocktail." The Modern Rogue, February 13, 2018. *themodernrogue.com*

Roséan, Lexa. *The Encyclopedia of Magickal Ingredients: A Wiccan Guide to Spellcasting*. London: Simon & Schuster, 2006.

Stewart, Amy. *The Drunken Botanist: The Plants that Create the World's Great Drinks*. London: Timber Press, 2015.

Stewart, Amy. *Wicked Plants: The Weed that Killed Lincoln's Mother & Other Botanical Atrocities*. Chapel Hill, NC: Algonquin Books of Chapel Hill, 2009.

Stott, Romie. "When Tomatoes Were Blamed for Witchcraft and Werewolves." *Atlas Obscura*. Atlas Obscura, November 14, 2016. *www.atlasobscura.com*

"Three Millennia of German Brewing." German Beer Institute 2005. Website, accessed March 15, 2020, is no longer working.

Wigington, Patti. "Magical Metals." Learn Religions. Accessed March 15, 2020. *www.learnreligions.com*

About the Author

Amy Blackthorn has a certification in aroma-therapy and incorporates her experiences in traditional witchcraft with her horticultural studies. Amy's company, Blackthorn Hoodoo Blends, creates tea based on old Hoodoo herbal formulas. Visit her at *www.amyblackthorn.com*.